Cambridge Elements

Elements in Publishing and Book Culture
edited by
Samantha J. Rayner
University College London
Leah Tether
University of Bristol

PAMPHLETEERING

Polemic, Print, and the Infrastructure of Political Agency

Pierre-Héli Monot
Ludwig Maximilian University of Munich

CAMBRIDGE
UNIVERSITY PRESS

Shaftesbury Road, Cambridge CB2 8EA, United Kingdom

One Liberty Plaza, 20th Floor, New York, NY 10006, USA

477 Williamstown Road, Port Melbourne, VIC 3207, Australia

314–321, 3rd Floor, Plot 3, Splendor Forum, Jasola District Centre,
New Delhi – 110025, India

103 Penang Road, #05–06/07, Visioncrest Commercial, Singapore 238467

Cambridge University Press is part of Cambridge University Press & Assessment,
a department of the University of Cambridge.

We share the University's mission to contribute to society through the pursuit of
education, learning and research at the highest international levels of excellence.

www.cambridge.org
Information on this title: www.cambridge.org/9781009550352

DOI: 10.1017/9781009550338

© Pierre-Héli Monot 2025

This publication is in copyright. Subject to statutory exception and to the provisions of relevant
collective licensing agreements, with the exception of the Creative Commons version the link for
which is provided below, no reproduction of any part may take place without the written permission
of Cambridge University Press & Assessment.

An online version of this work is published at doi.org/10.1017/9781009550338 under a Creative
Commons Open Access license CC-BY-NC 4.0 which permits re-use, distribution and reproduction
in any medium for non-commercial purposes providing appropriate credit to the original work is
given and any changes made are indicated. To view a copy of this license visit
https://creativecommons.org/licenses/by-nc/4.0

When citing this work, please include a reference to the DOI 10.1017/9781009550338

First published 2025

A catalogue record for this publication is available from the British Library

ISBN 978-1-009-55035-2 Paperback
ISSN 2514-8524 (online)
ISSN 2514-8516 (print)

Cambridge University Press & Assessment has no responsibility for the persistence or accuracy of
URLs for external or third-party internet websites referred to in this publication and does not guarantee
that any content on such websites is, or will remain, accurate or appropriate.

For EU product safety concerns, contact us at Calle de José Abascal, 56, 1°, 28003 Madrid, Spain, or
email eugpsr@cambridge.org

Pamphleteering

Polemic, Print, and the Infrastructure of Political Agency

Elements in Publishing and Book Culture

DOI: 10.1017/9781009550338
First published online: September 2025

Pierre-Héli Monot
Ludwig Maximilian University of Munich

Author for correspondence: Pierre-Héli Monot, p.monot@lmu.de

ABSTRACT: The 'Pamphlet Wars' of the seventeenth century, the activist texts of the Labour Movement, and the recent campaigns for climate justice have all drawn on the affordances of pamphleteering to advance their cause: pamphlets circulate across geographical boundaries and social divides, they attract a readership that is usually excluded from the classical public sphere, they can be produced at low cost, and they often provide anonymity to their authors. This Element provides a brief history of short-form polemical literature from the Reformation to the present. It argues that popular dissent and popular political agency must be understood in light of the material and, more recently, digital history of polemical literature. It makes the case that current online polemic is best understood as a late infrastructural transformation of classical and modern pamphleteering. This title is also available as Open Access on Cambridge Core.

KEYWORDS: pamphlet, literature, political history, book history, polemic

© Pierre-Héli Monot 2025

ISBNs: 9781009550352 (PB), 9781009550338 (OC)
ISSNs: 2514-8524 (online), 2514-8516 (print)

Contents

1 Introduction 1

2 Infrastructure: From Antiquity to the Printing Press 5

3 'Ordinary Readers': Revolutionary Pamphleteering 18

4 Beneath the Public Sphere: Radical Pamphleteering 1898–1950 28

5 The Civil Rights Movement: A Pamphletary Event 49

6 Pamphleteering after Paper 70

Bibliography 82

1 Introduction

Seen from a historical distance, the global archive of pamphletary literature sometimes resembles a towering mass of discontent, dissent, despair, social aspirations, political creativity, thwarted hopes, linguistic obscenity, and political desires.[1] No other literary tradition displays quite the same political intensity as that to be found at the core of polemical texts. This is hardly surprising, given the stakes at play whenever authors and readers turn to short-form polemical literature to enforce justice, demand rights, or affirm dignity.[2]

Since the advent of the printing press in the late fifteenth century, pamphlets have been at the forefront of major philosophical, social, and political transformations. Pamphlets have accompanied and sometimes directly triggered processes of democratization or fascization, colonization or decolonization, the universalization of civil and civic rights, the enforcement of political or territorial autonomy, the protracted abolition of slavery across the globe, the development of socialized medicine, and the critique of labour exploitation and gender inequality. Pamphlets have also had a massive influence on the development of general readerships across the globe, allowing populations to participate in political processes in increasingly complex social and political settings. The 'Pamphlet Wars' of the seventeenth century, the activist texts of the Labour Movement, and the recent campaigns for climate justice have all drawn on the affordances of pamphleteering to advance their cause: pamphlets circulate across geographical boundaries and social divides, they reach and attract a readership that is usually excluded from the genteel public sphere, they can be produced at low cost, and they often provide anonymity to their authors. The pamphlet

---

[1] J den Hollander, H. Paul, R. Peters, 'Introduction: The Metaphor of Historical Distance', *History and Theory*, vol. 50, no. 4 (December 2011), pp. 1–10, 1.

[2] This project has received funding from the European Research Council (ERC) under the European Union's Horizon 2020 research and innovation programme (grant agreement No 852205). This publication reflects only the author's view, and the Agency is not responsible for any use that may be made of the information it contains.

is part not only of the fabric of Modernity, but also of many of its greatest accomplishments and worst transgressions.

Seen from the vantage point of literary history, philology, social history, and book history – that is, seen from a *scholastic* vantage point – the pamphlet raises a set of vexing questions and has done so since the professionalization of literary studies at the turn of the twentieth century. When did readers and writers begin endowing polemical texts with the ability to transform social relations? How were these texts produced and how did they circulate in the first place? How were they received by an audience that was almost always politically vulnerable, often persecuted, and sometimes illiterate? How did the police surveillance of polemical literature affect its contents? How should scholars define 'the pamphlet' as a literary object, given the extreme heterogeneity of its formal features and ideological dispositions across history? Does it make sense to think of polemical statements posted on social media as 'digital pamphlets' or 'postprint pamphlets'? Scholastic reason, in short, has long failed to take the full measure of this crucial literary tradition. Not a single general literary history of pamphleteering has ever been published, despite the centrality of pamphlets in most literary cultures. The fact that open letters, manifestos, pamphlets, and tracts constitute a major segment of the global literary archive is barely recognized in the standard anthologies of literature. Nor is there any recent theory of polemical literature, despite intense discussions about the place of activism and partisanship in literary and academic cultures.

This short book wants to make a few basic claims that, in turn, should answer some of the questions raised above and help alleviate the long-standing academic neglect of the pamphlet. In what follows, I want above all to make three interdependent, mutually enlightening points:

1. Pamphleteering is best thought of not as a clearly defined literary form, format, or style, but rather as a social practice that engages one or several authors, a readership, and a clearly identified sociopolitical context or normative horizon. Pamphleteering is a collective activity that societies turn to in specific historical circumstances. This Element therefore proposes a pragmatic definition of pamphleteering that

emphasizes its *social uses* rather than its *literary form* or *political content*. While this approach perhaps overly broadens the classical definition of the pamphlet, it does so affirmatively and rigorously: in order to be considered as pamphlets, polemical texts must have been the object of wide circulation and intense public controversy. Polemical texts that do not meet these criteria fall outside of the scope of this Element.

2. Pamphleteering depends on a specific *infrastructure*, that is, large-scale techniques of reproduction ranging from the printing press to digital networks. For pamphlets to unfold their political power and become the object of collective practices, they need to circulate using particular infrastructural means and following particular socio-political routes. While other printed media traditionally circulates in a way that roughly corresponds to the outline of the public sphere, pamphlets use mass *reproduction* and *circulation* to bypass established circuits and reach populations that are excluded from the public sphere and its discursive expectations. In doing so, pamphlets make literature observable as a social fact.

3. Consequently, the development of a *popular political agency*, understood as broadly distributed means to participate both discursively and practically in the elaboration and attainment of desired political goals, is dependent on a specific media infrastructure. Put differently, while writing, reading, and circulating polemical texts has been a crucial activity for populations since Antiquity, it is only since the generalization of the printing press that populations have been able to consistently exert political pressure using texts. This, in turn, can be rephrased as a disciplinary argument: Book History has something to say not only about the development of polemical literature, but also about the popular uses of political power since the Reformation. Book History is, or could be, a history of the political power attributed to books.

This Element is divided into five main sections that are organized chronologically. Each section aims to accomplish three things: it briefly introduces a *historical phase*, it outlines a set of *theoretical or conceptual questions*, and it analyses *specific textual examples*. Along the way, this Element makes several arguments for renewed attention to be paid to the importance of

Book History for political history. While this Element cannot provide a general and transnational history of pamphleteering and its publics, and while it must ignore crucial texts and political movements, I hope the argument it makes will further consolidate the growing scholarly interest in confrontational literary discourse, its infrastructures, and its effects on political history.

Note: The titles of all pamphlets discussed in this Element are italicized in order improve legibility and eschew ambiguities in categorization and literary taxonomy. Since 2020, my work has been supported by the ERC Starting Grant *The Arts of Autonomy: Pamphleteering, Popular Philology, and the Public Sphere*. Some of the texts discussed in this Element have been the object of much more sustained inquiry in other formats. Some have been the object of series of preliminary texts, white papers, and open-access beta versions of critical editions. The Element systematizes and historicizes some of these preliminary findings in a concise manner. While some repetitions in argumentation and wording are unavoidable, I encourage readers to consult our many open-access publications for additional material.

2 Infrastructure: From Antiquity to the Printing Press

2.1 Polemic before Pamphleteering

Polemic, political agitation, and ad hominem attacks have left important written traces in all scribal and manuscript cultures reaching as far back as ancient Sumer and the Middle Kingdom of Egypt.[3] These texts often contested the legitimacy of rulers, called the impartiality of judges into question, and sometimes engaged in heretic speculations about the nature or existence of divinities. Yet why are literary historians usually reluctant to describe these texts as pamphlets in the usual, colloquial, hence ahistorical sense of the term? Consider the following two examples from ancient Egypt and fifth-century-BCE China.

In the Egyptian tale *The Eloquent Peasant* (*Sekhti-nefer-medu*, 1850 BCE), the poor peasant Khun-Anup petitions the high steward Rensi to receive justice in a case involving donkeys stolen by Nemtynakht, a subordinate of Rensi. In the nine impassioned petitions that make up the bulk of the tale, Khun-Anup develops a theory of ordinary or vulgar justice[4] that indirectly accuses his rulers Rensi, the Pharaoh Nebkaure, and the magistrates of the Middle Kingdom: 'The arbitrator is a robber, the remover of need orders its creation, the town is a floodwater, the punisher of evil commits crimes!'[5] Yet instead of being sentenced to death for his accusations, Khun-Anup is rewarded for his rhetorical feats: the literary qualities of Khun-Anup's petitions are praised so highly by the Pharaoh that neither his legal transgressions nor his rhetorical offenses incur punishment.

In the *Book of Mozi* (墨子), written during the Warring States period (476–221 BCE), Master Mo[6] violently attacks Confucianism which, by the end of the third century, had begun evolving into an official state

---

[3] Earlier preserved texts generally consist of didactic literature and theological treatises. The focus here is on texts that do not fit these clearly defined literary categories.

[4] See for instance: A. David, 'The *nmḥ* and the Paradox of the Voiceless in *The Eloquent Peasant*', *The Journal of Egyptian Archaeology*, vol. 97 (2011), pp. 73–85, 82.

[5] Anonymous, 'The Eloquent Peasant', M. Lichtheim, ed., *Ancient Egyptian Literature*, (University of California Press, 2019), pp. 214–292, 219.

[6] Master Mo is also known as Mo Tzu, Mozi, Mo Zi, Mo Tse, Mo Di, and Micius.

philosophy. Chapter 39 in particular contains a series of personal attacks against Confucius, extensive use of incestuous wordplay, animalistic insults, and a sharp critique of Confucianism as a philosophical and political proposition: 'Confucianism', Master Mo summarizes, 'is damaging to the people of the world'.[7] Neither the complete text of the *Book of Mozi*, nor the philosophical tradition it engendered (*Mohism*) survived China's 'philosophical dark age'[8] inaugurated by the hegemony of Confucianism. Yet the *Book of Mozi* did have a later use as a political text: it was held in high esteem by Mao Zedong, who called Master Mo the 'Chinese Heraclitus'[9] and thought the text well-attuned to the ideological mainstays of the Cultural Revolution. In the *Mozi*, Mao found an ally in his rhetorical war against the staunch conservatism and pietism of Confucianism.[10]

What these two texts have in common is that they failed to circulate widely enough to escape political capture. While *The Eloquent Peasant* was preserved on no fewer than four distinct papyri[11] and can therefore be thought to have circulated widely among the literate population of the Middle Kingdom, its fate depended on the good will and personal interests of professional scribes, copyists, collectors, literate patrons, and owners. Conversely, the *Mozi* was effectively suppressed for two millennia before it was rediscovered as an instrument of revolutionary statecraft. Like most polemical texts written during Antiquity, these texts survived not as

---

[7] Mo Zi, *The Book of Master Mo*, ed. I. Johnston, (Penguin, 2013), p. 190.

[8] C. Hansen, *A Daoist Theory of Chinese Thought: A Philosophical Interpretation*, (Oxford University Press, 1992), p. 96.

[9] Mao Zedong, 'Letter to Chen Boda, February 1, 1939', in Mao Zedong, S. R. Schram, ed., *Mao's Road to Power: Revolutionary Writings, 1912–1949*, Volume VII, *New Democracy: 1939–1941*, (M. E. Sharpe, 2004), p. 22.

[10] I have written at greater length about the *Book of Mozi* in: P.-H. Monot, ed., 'The Book of Mozi: Chapter 39. "Against the Confucians" (Fei Ru Xia). A Commented Edition with Contextual Sources' (Version 1.0), in P.-H. Monot, ed., *The Arts of Autonomy: A Living Anthology of Polemical Literature*, (The Arts of Autonomy, 2022), pp. 1–18.

[11] N. Shupak, 'A New Source for the Study of the Judiciary and Law of Ancient Egypt: "The Tale of the Eloquent Peasant"', *Journal of near Eastern Studies*, vol. 51, no. 1 (January 1992), pp. 1–18, 2.

polemic, but as religious doctrine, literature, state propaganda, or philosophy, all understood as social practices largely controlled and administered by particularly affluent and powerful social groups. Lacking adequate means of reproduction and circulation and failing to reach a popular social basis beyond the gates of governance and amateur philology, polemical texts generally failed to unleash a political power in any way comparable to their political ambitions.

Contrast *The Eloquent Peasant* and the *Book of Mozi* with a crucial counterexample that marks the gradual emergence of a specific system of circulation for polemical texts. In *The Clouds* (Νεφέλαι, *Nephelai*, 423 BCE), Aristophanes levels several grave accusations against Socrates. The philosopher is said to corrupt the Athenian youth and to deny the very existence of the gods. More importantly, Socrates is accused of teaching discursive techniques by which citizens might evade their financial, ethical, and political duties, thereby impacting the whole economic fate of the city. By pointing out the social uses of Socrates' purportedly nefarious teachings in a commerce-oriented city whose population exceeded 250,000 inhabitants,[12] *The Clouds* makes philosophy the urgent concern of the entire political and economic community: the play concerns not only the philosopher in particular, but also the city in general.

Did *The Clouds* really contribute to the mounting resentment felt by prominent Athenians towards Socrates, as is often alleged? In fact, if Aristophanes' other comedies usually failed to shape public opinion, *The Clouds* was a significant exception. It was arguably written *for readers*, rather than for a theatrical audience, and it had an identifiable literary transmission,[13] thereby indicating a crucial shift from an oral to an increasingly literary, text-oriented culture in Athens. *The Clouds*, in other words, had a social existence as a kind of pre-modern polemical text, revealing the close relationship between the circulation of literary statements, the growing involvement of the 'city' as an object of common political concern, and the progressive emergence of a culture of efficient literary slander against individuals. Once texts were copied

---

[12] J. Ober, *The Rise and Fall of Classical Greece*, (Princeton University Press, 2015), pp. 204–206.

[13] R. M. Rosen, 'Performance and Textuality in Aristophanes' Clouds', *The Yale Journal of Criticism*, vol. 10, no. 2 (1997), pp. 397–421, 397.

and brought to circulate among the population, they were found to wield a uniquely treacherous kind of political power, as Plato repeatedly deplores.[14] Political and philosophical campaigns against opponents and competitors could be mounted with little more than a sheet of papyrus, an audience inclined to public polemic, and a set of common political or economic stakes. At the same time Athens discovered the affordances of writing for the administration of commerce and the law, it discovered its affordances and risks as a tool for the pursuit of power. Literature was henceforth perceived to hold a distinct political force: it misled judgment, disseminated slander against individuals, and could be brought to bear on legal proceedings. In fact, the jurors of 399 BCE were too young have attended the original performance of *The Clouds*. Yet the play seems to have been on the jurors' minds, attesting to changing perception of polemical literature in Antiquity.[15]

2.2 A Pamphletary Infrastructure

By reproducing polemical texts, scribes and copyists made them accessible to a growing number of readers in an increasingly wide range of social contexts. Statements made in a theatrical setting could now be decontextualized and used as statements of fact in a criminal trial: writing, in other words, made social context contingent. This central affordance of writing must be understood as an *infrastructural* transformation in the history of polemic. Once put to papyrus, accusations and satire gained the advantage of being *iterable* and *socially mobile*: they could be reproduced, albeit in relatively small quantities, and circulated within several local and institutional contexts at the same time.[16]

---

[14] Plato even discreetly hints at the problems posed by writing in the dialogues concerned with the trial of Socrates, notably in the *Apology*.

[15] I am here condensing an argument I made in: P.-H. Monot, ed., 'Aristophanes: *The Clouds*. A Commented Edition with Contextual Sources, Translated by Ian Johnston' (Version 1.0), in P.-H. Monot, ed., *The Arts of Autonomy: A Living Anthology of Polemical Literature*, (The Arts of Autonomy, 2024), pp. 1–121. Some repetitions in phrasing are unavoidable.

[16] Very generally, see: C. Levine, *Forms: Whole, Rhythm, Hierarchy, Network*, (Princeton University Press, 2015), p. 7.

Importantly, this affordance was at first a 'hidden affordance', that is, one that was discovered by secondary social actors, rather than by the original addressees.[17] The unfolding of a specific political power attached to written polemic was an unexpected offshoot of Greek scribal culture that, in turn, triggered a set of energetic responses seeking to contain the most disruptive effects of polemical texts. In other words, the discovery of the political affordances of writing inaugurated one of the few relative constants in the history of polemical writing. Beginning with scribal cultures and leading up to current digital publics and counterpublics, this historical constant can best be described as an asymmetry between established institutional powers and the infrastructural means of reproduction and circulation of pamphletary writing, from manuscript copies to mimeographs, samizdats, radical imprints, and weblogs.

Very simply put, this asymmetry was detrimental to polemical authors and publics up until the generalization of the printing press and the European Reformation in the early sixteenth century: outright polemic was usually perceived as either overly risky or insufficiently effective. Before the major infrastructural transformations brought about by the printing industry, the disproportion between the affordance of manuscript copies on the one hand, and the slow emergence of state[18] and protocapitalist[19] structures, the globalization of trade networks,[20] the codification of legal frameworks,[21] the appearance of bureaucratic

---

[17] I am here drawing on an important distinction in design theory otherwise absent in Levine's influential account. William W. Gaver explains: 'If there is no information available for an existing affordance, it is hidden and must be inferred from other evidence'. W. H. Gaver, 'Technological Affordances', *Proceedings of CHI'91*, (New Orleans, Louisiana, 28 April–2 May 1991), ACM, New York, pp. 79–84, 80.

[18] J. R. Strayer, *On the Medieval Origins of the Modern State*, (Princeton University Press, 2005).

[19] B. R. Scott, *Capitalism: Its Origins and Evolution as a System of Governance*, (Springer, 2011), pp. 141–184.

[20] G. Heng, *The Global Middle Ages: An Introduction*, (Cambridge University Press, 2021).

[21] S. Wolin, *Politics and Vision: Continuity and Innovation in Western Political Thought*, (Princeton University Press, 2016), pp. 143–163.

institutions,[22] the differentiation of social classes and milieus[23] on the other hand, usually made written contestation both risky and futile.

There were of course several notable exceptions. The manuscript material that accompanied Proto-Protestant movements in Europe (the Wycliffite heresies in England from the 1370s onwards, for instance[24]), the medieval polemics against Islam (Riccoldo da Monte di Croce's *Contra Legem Sarracenorum*, 1300[25]), and the nascent genre of the antisemitic blood libel (Thomas of Monmouth's *Vita et Passione Sancti Willelmi Martyris Norwicensis*, second half of the twelfth century[26]) undoubtedly played a crucial role in shaping cultures of invective, critique, and calumny in their respective eras and contexts. Yet it is the printing press that allowed a more general culture of articulating conflict and dissent to emerge in early modern Europe, reversing the asymmetry between instituted powers and polemical counterpublics.[27]

In fact, the production of pamphlets and broadsheets was a mainstay of the printing trade from the beginning, only surpassed in numbers by the indulgences printed on behalf of an enormous range of religious institutions (confraternities, churches, parishes, monasteries, etc.; see Figure 1). The sheer magnitude of this industry is worth considering. In 1480 alone, Augsburg printer Johan Bämler printed 12,000 letters of indulgence. In the same city and that same year, Jodocus Pflanzmann printed 20,000 certificates of confession.[28] The numbers would keep increasing well into

---

[22] M. Weber, *Economy and Society*, vol. 2, ed. G. Roth and C. Wittrich, (University of California Press, 1978), pp. 956–1001.

[23] S. H. Rigby, *English Society in the Later Middle Ages: Class, Status, Gender*, (Macmillan, 1995).

[24] K. Ghosh, *The Wycliffite Heresies: Authority and the Interpretation of Texts*, (Cambridge University Press, 2004).

[25] J. V. Tolan, *Saracens: Islam in the Medieval European Imagination*, (Columbia University Press, 2002).

[26] H. Blurton, *Inventing William of Norwich: Thomas of Monmouth, Antisemitism, and Literary Culture, 1150–1200*, (University of Pennsylvania Press, 2022).

[27] I will clarify the use of the concepts of 'publics' and 'counterpublics' in Section 3.3.

[28] P. Stallybrass, '"Little Jobs": Broadsides and the Printing Revolution', S. A. Baron, E. N. Lindqvist, E. F. Shevlin, eds., *Agent of Change: Print Culture*

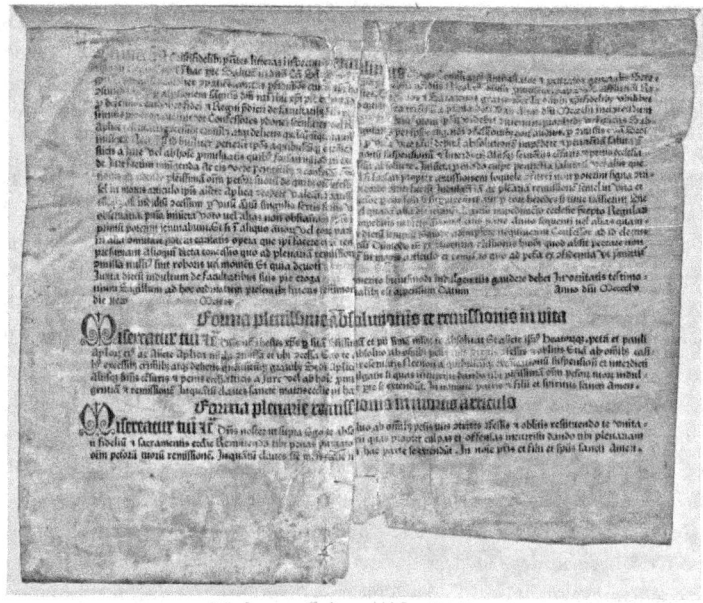

Figure 1 Printed Cyprus Indulgence, 31 lines. Mainz: Johann Gutenberg, 1454. 1 vellum leaf; 21 x 26 cm. Incunabula at Princeton, courtesy of Princeton University Library.

the pre-Reformation period: in 1499–1500, Johann Luscher's workshop churned out 142,950 indulgences, with other printers setting up additional workshops to cope with the demand.[29]

Studies after Elizabeth L. Eisenstein, (University of Massachusetts Press, 2007), pp. 315–341, 316.

[29] I am summarizing from: P. Stallybrass, 'Everyday Objects', in J. Symonds, ed., *A Cultural History of Objects in the Renaissance*, (Bloomsbury Academic, 2021), pp. 103–124, 119.

These formats responded to an urgent economic necessity. Gutenberg's work on the Latin Vulgate Bible, for instance, begun soon after 1450 and making first copies available in 1454/1455, depended on enormous and continuous investments in paper that would contribute to his effective bankruptcy by the mid-1450s. The production of indulgences, along with calendars, sensationalized Christian hagiographies, ballads, and broadsheets (advertisements and announcements printed on one side only), ensured both rapid cash-flow for German printers and a degree of leniency from the ecclesiastical authorities.[30] In turn, the near-industrial production of indulgences made the 'trafficking in salvation'[31] attractive to the Catholic Church which hoped to finance herculean projects such as the rebuilding of St. Beter's Basilica in Rome and a new crusade against the Turks.[32] The absolution of penitent sinners, the production of indulgences via movable type, and the subsidizing of large-scale projects via the mass reproduction of ecclesiastical texts went hand in hand, establishing a three-fold moral, political, and monetary economy around the early printing revolution.

This 'economy of salvation'[33] must be supplemented with what can perhaps best be described as an 'economy of dissent' which arose in its immediate wake. Martin Luther's *Ninety-Five Theses* or *Disputation on the Power and Efficacy of Indulgences*, which he may have posted on the door of All Saints' Church in Wittenberg[34] in 1517, was the first volley in a long pamphlet war which ultimately brought about the Reformation (see

---

[30] On broadsheets, see: A. Pettegree, ed., *Broadsheets: Single-Sheet Publishing in the First Age of Print*, (Brill, 2017).

[31] E. L. Eisenstein, *The Printing Press as an Agent of Change: Communications and Cultural Transformations in Early-Modern Europe*, (Cambridge University Press, 1997), p. 375.

[32] See Johann Tetzel below.

[33] A. Pettegree, *Brand Luther: How an Unheralded Monk Turned His Small Town into a Center of Publishing, Made Himself the Most Famous Man in Europe – and Started the Protestant Reformation*, (Penguin, 2015), 55.

[34] Although there is some doubt about its historical accuracy, the act of posting theses on every church door in Wittenberg would have been in accordance with university customs.

Figure 2 1517 Nuremberg placard edition of Martin Luther's *Ninety-five Theses*. Courtesy of Stabi Berlin. <http://resolver.staatsbibliothek-berlin.de/SBB00003DCA00000000>

Figure 2). Luther, then a junior professor of moral theology in Wittenberg, directly attacked the commerce of indulgences:

> *Thesis 32*: Those who believe that they can be certain of their salvation because they have indulgence letters will be eternally damned, together with their teachers.
>
> *Thesis 43*: Christians are to be taught that he who gives to the poor or lends to the needy does a better deed than he who buys indulgences.[35]

Writing for 'a love for the truth and a desire to elucidate it',[36] Luther would engender a long tradition of metaphysical-political claims that would profoundly influence the rhetoric of pamphleteering well into the twentieth century (the word 'truth' itself, for instance, appears eighteen times in Émile Zola's 1898 pamphlet *J'Accuse . . . !*[37]). The *generality* acquired by pamphlets during the Reformation therefore made it possible and necessary for polemical claims to become staples of public discourse, rather than being confined to theological disputes. Let me briefly break down the advent of pamphleteering as society-at-large discourse into three main points.

First, Luther's sweeping indictment of the specific religious practice of indulgences had decidedly general effects, setting off a pamphlet war between innumerable individual and institutional parties, most famously Johann Tetzel, then Grand Commissioner for Indulgences, whose *106 Theses* (orig.: *Vorlegung*, 1518) were printed barely six months after Luther's own.[38] Between 1500 and 1530, more than 10,000 individual pamphlets were printed in Germany alone,[39] establishing key formal features by way of strict economic

---

[35] M. Luther, 'The Ninety-Five Theses: A Disputation to Clarify the Power of Indulgences', in W. R. Russell, ed., *The Ninety-Five Theses and Other Writings*, (Penguin, 2017), pp. 1–13, 6–7.

[36] Ibid, p. 3.   [37] I will return to Zola in section 4.1.

[38] D. W. Kramer, ed., *Johann Tetzel's Rebuttal against Luther's Sermon on Indulgences and Grace*, (Pitts Theology Library, 2012), pp. 1–32.

[39] A. Pettegree, 'Books, Pamphlets and Polemic', A. Pettegree, ed., *The Reformation World*, (Routledge, 2000), pp. 109–126, p. 110.

opportunity: pamphlets were brief (usually two sheets at most), they were printed in large editions of hundreds or thousands, they were affordable or distributed for free, and they circulated widely among the population. Between 1518 and 1526, an estimated 6,000,000 pamphlets were printed.[40]

Second, the generality of their claims made texts such as Luther's *Ninety-five Theses* the concern not only of ecclesiastical authorities, but of the entire fabric of literate society: criticism of the commerce of indulgences was not only a point of religious doctrine, but it also implicated the material, political, and moral economies of the Church, the printing industry, and the body politic of the region (see Figure 3). Taking note of pamphletary production – and often responding to pamphlets by either publishing other pamphlets or imposing coercive measures – became a political imperative for the authorities and the literate population alike.[41] The co-dependency of the development of print infrastructures in Europe, the emergence of an increasingly educated concern for politics among the laity, and the consolidation of organs of censorship must therefore be emphasized. In fact, the sheer mass of polemical publications issued by printing operations of all sizes would render null and void most localized coercive measures in Germany, ranging from regional censorship to prohibition, as early as the early seventeenth century.[42]

Third, and in line with this last point, the pamphlet helped establish an early, properly *public* sphere, the development of which will be the focus of the next section. In the *Theses*, Luther discovered a popular voice and dispensed with elaborate terminology,[43] thereby emphasizing the

---

[40] Jarvis summarizes Pettegree and others in: J. Jarvis, *The Gutenberg Parenthesis: The Age of Print and its Lessons for the Age of the Internet*, (Bloomsbury Academic, 2023), p. 68.

[41] See also: P.-H. Monot, 'Art, Autonomy, Philology: Project Parameters', in P.-H. Monot, D. Bebnowski, S. Gröppmaier, eds., *Activist Writing: History, Politics, Rhetoric*, (Intercom, 2024), pp. 16–23.

[42] I am summarizing W. Burgdorf, 'Der intergouvernementale publizistische Diskurs. Agitation und Emanzipation, politische Gelegenheitsschriften und ihre Bedeutung für die Entstehung politischer Öffentlichkeit im Alten Reich', in J. Arndt, E.-B. Körber, eds., *Das Mediensystem im Alten Reich der Frühen Neuzeit (1600–1750)*, (Vandenhoeck & Ruprecht, 2010), pp. 75–98, 77.

[43] A. Pettegree, *The French Book and the European Book World*, (Brill, 2007), 224.

Figure 3 Bertold of Regensburg, vernacular sermon in German. *Sermones Germanici*, manuscript, 1444. Courtesy of the Austrian National Library. <http://data.onb.ac.at/rec/AC13951319>

'conversational'[44] nature of the pamphlet as a new type of media. The hundreds of copies of the Latin *Theses*, their translation into German by Kaspar Nützel a few months later, their extraordinary circulation in a matter of months (first to the Catholic centres of Augsburg and Ingolstadt, then across Germany, then across Switzerland,[45] finally across much of

[44] J. Jarvis, *The Gutenberg Parenthesis*, 68.
[45] J. Schilling, 'Einleitung', in M. Luther, J. Schilling, eds., *Christusglaube und Rechtfertigung*, (Evangelische Verlagsanstalt, 2006), pp. ix–xxxix, p. x.

Europe[46]), as well as the incipient standardization of German in countless derivative publications (Johannes Pollicarius' bestselling biographical pamphlet about Luther[47]) made 'the poor' and 'the needy' (Thesis 43) not only the object of Luther's theological dispute, but also its virtual addressees.

By the late sixteenth century, the pamphlet was firmly established across Europe as a type of media, as a politico-religious activity, and as a source of incessant worry for the authorities. While the myth of Luther galvanizing an entire continent by way of vernacular polemic perhaps looms overly large in the history of literacy research, literacy rates did increase spectacularly during the period (from about 5 per cent of the population in Germany and Britain in 1450 to about 16 per cent in 1550, although such estimates pose as many problems as they attempt to solve).[48] The decline of classical rhetoric, the development of the book trade, and the spread of vernacular scripture[49] further set the scene for two ensuing centuries of radical pamphleteering.

---

[46] R. Rex, *The Making of Martin Luther*, (Princeton University Press, 2017), 11.

[47] V. Leppin and T. J. Wengert, 'Sources for and against the Posting of the Ninety-Five Theses', *Lutheran Quarterly*, vol. 29 (2015), pp. 373–398.

[48] P. Crain, 'New Histories of Literacy', in S. Eliot, J. Rose, eds., *A Companion to the History of the Book*, vol. 1, (Wiley, 2019), pp. 143–156.

[49] J. Raymond, *Pamphlets and Pamphleteering in Early Modern Britain*, (Cambridge University Press, 2003), p. 11.

3 'Ordinary Readers': Revolutionary Pamphleteering

3.1 The Pamphlet as Event

What, then, is a 'pamphlet'? All at once a format, a genre, a rhetorical style, and a type of media, the pamphlet has consistently eluded attempts at a transhistorical definition. Historians of the pamphlet, encyclopaedias, and pamphleteers themselves have either pointed out material generalities (a 'short handwritten work or document of several pages fastened together; a handwritten poem, tract, or treatise',[50] a 'short piece of polemical writing'[51] of 'ephemeral duration'[52]), or universalized highly localized practices (for Nicholas Thoburn, pamphlets are primarily 'communist objects'[53]), or emphasized the confrontational nature of pamphletary texts (pamphlets as 'agitational objects'[54] or simply as 'violent and aggressive texts'[55]).

Without overcomplicating matters, these definitions routinely neglect the extraordinary diversity of pamphletary writing. Many canonical pamphlets fail to match its core taxonomic features: Zola's *J'Accuse ... !* was published in a newspaper as an open letter, Ted Kaczynski's *Industrial Society and its Future* (also known as *The Unabomber Manifesto*) is

---

[50] Oxford English Dictionary, s.v. 'pamphlet (n.), sense 1.a', September 2024, https://doi.org/10.1093/OED/7633100455.

[51] G. Orwell, 'Introduction', G. Orwell, R. Reynolds, eds., *British Pamphleteers. Volume 1, from the Sixteenth Century to the French Revolution*, (London: Allan Wingate, 1948), pp. 7–17, p. 7.

[52] N. Thoburn, 'Communist Objects and the Values of Printed Matter', *Social Text*, vol. 28/2, no. 103 (Summer 2010), pp. 1–30, p. 11.

[53] Ibid., pp. 1–30.

[54] G. Whiteley : 'The Allure of *Pamphilos*: The Radical Art of Pamphleteering', in J. Tormey, G. Whiteley, eds., *Art, Politics, and the Pamphleteer*, (Bloomsbury Academic, 2021), p. 6.

[55] '*textes violents et agressifs*', my translation. M. Hastings, C. Passard, J. Rennes, 'Les mutations du pamphlet dans la France contemporaine', *Mots: Les langages du politique* vol. 91 (2009), pp. 5–17, p. 5. P.-H. Monot, 'Pretty Pamphlets', in P.-H. Monot, D. Bebnowski, S. Gröppmaier, eds., *Activist Writing: History, Politics, Rhetoric*, (Intercom, 2024), p. 68.

significantly longer than the Element you are currently reading, and countless nominal 'pamphlets' circulate poorly, if at all. Conversely, commercial imprints have recently launched series that exclusively publish inexpensive, short, polemical, pseudo-pamphletary texts that nonetheless fail to elicit public interest, let alone trigger a 'pamphlet war'.[56]

The salient feature of all texts usually considered to be pamphlets is that they set a very specific *social response* in motion. Whenever short-form polemic successfully operates *as* a pamphlet, rather than as a philosophical polemic (the *Book of Mozi*), literature (*The Eloquent Peasant*), or religious ephemera (short-form Christian hagiographies), they call a reading public into being and trigger historically specific containment measures from public authorities. Pamphlets are always an event that takes place in the public sphere as much as in its margins. In this section, I will briefly theorize the practical contours of pamphleteering as a social event by way of a discussion of revolutionary polemic in eighteenth-century France and the United States.

3.2 Surveilling Readerships

The commonly assumed and almost certainly inaccurate[57] etymology of the term 'pamphlet' should provide a hint at what the pamphlet does *not* do: in name, the *pan-philos* should be loved by all, interrupt belligerent discourse, and reassert common political interests.[58] Etymologically, the pamphlet should reassure readers that, if nothing else, they at least have a love of polemical discourse in common. Indeed, the slow generalization and

---

[56] Gallimard (France) launched the 'Tracts' series in 2019. Nautilus (Germany) has translated many of the notorious pamphlets of the 2000s. See also: B. Bréville, 'Pétitionnaires de tous les pays . . . ', *Le Monde diplomatique* (August 2020), p. 28.

[57] Y. Bellenger, 'Le pamphlet avant le pamphlet: le mot et la chose', *Cahiers de l'Association International des Études Françaises*, vol. 36 (1984), pp. 87–96.

[58] G. Whiteley : 'The Allure of *Pamphilos*: The Radical Art of Pamphleteering', in J. Tormey, G. Whiteley, eds., *Art, Politics, and the Pamphleteer*, (Bloomsbury Academic, 2021), p. 6. I am summarizing a longer essay on this question: P.-H. Monot, 'Pretty Pamphlets', in P.-H. Monot, D. Bebnowski, S. Gröppmaier, eds., *Activist Writing: History, Politics, Rhetoric*, (Intercom, 2024), pp. 68–82.

formalization of a satirical, ironic, indirect, and indiscreet tone in polemical writing from Thomas Dekker to Jonathan Swift bolstered the respectability of pamphletary writing: from the late seventeenth century onwards, short-form polemic was increasingly read in the salons, coffee houses, and reading circles of polite society. Some historical pamphlets also gained in longevity, prestige, and accessibility. Perhaps most canonically, Jack Cade's *The Complaint of the Poor Commons of Kent* (1450) was adapted into popular diatribes in Shakespeare's *Henry VI, Part 2* (1591).

Despite these factors, the oppositional logic of the pamphlet has almost always fractured extant reading publics, polarizing segments of the reading population into distinct, often radicalized subgroups. In fact, everywhere across Europe and the British Isles, popular dissent was brewing, pitting social groups against one another. The loosening of censorship during the British Civil Wars saw the publication of 20,000 pamphlets and polemical books,[59] while printing and circulation circuits for polemical literature were consolidated throughout Germany and France. Perhaps even more clearly than during the Reformation, pamphleteering in the seventeenth and early eighteenth centuries – a relative lacuna in many European prose literatures – brought about a social dynamic of mutual radicalization among readerships. In turn, oppositional reading publics would be forced to argue for their positions on either rational or rhetorical grounds.[60]

This sits somewhat uneasily alongside the paradigm of a 'public sphere', whose emergence Jürgen Habermas locates during the early Enlightenment. Habermas's account (first published in 1962) emphasizes the joint development of the European bourgeoisie as a social class, the emergence of a learned culture in salons and coffee houses, and the saturation of public discourse and public opinion by a proliferation of daily publications ushering in an era of deliberative rationality among European populations. While in pre-bourgeois times the 'public sphere'

---

[59] J. Holstun, 'Introduction', in J. Holstun, ed., *Pamphlet Wars: Prose in the English Revolution*, (Frank Cass, 1992), pp. 1–13, p. 6.

[60] On this historical distinction see: C. Castoriadis, *The Imaginary Institution of Society*, (MIT Press, 1987), pp. 185–208.

had been generally 'co-extensive with public authority',[61] that is, the State, it was now co-extensive with a specific subject position which remained implicit in Habermas's account: the readers who presided over 'public opinion' were male, bourgeois, often Christian, and always literate. Here, the social structure of the public sphere functioned as an objective gate-keeper: the potential access to texts, and therefore to political agency, was congruent with the degree of affiliation to the male, Christian, affluent, and literate bourgeoisie. In Habermas's account, the very ideals of the bourgeois public sphere – its pretension to universality, above all – were contradicted by its material, political, and moral organization.[62]

Yet on the margins of bourgeois readership, popular literacies not only flourished, but also began raising concrete problems of governance for State power and routinely overtaxed the tolerance of bourgeois publics for libellous writings. Some pre-revolutionary pamphlets were in fact so pornographic and so widely circulated that they horrified the very Enlightenment figures who had supported free speech and public rationality in the first place.[63] The resulting exclusionary[64] effects of the Habermasian public sphere were supplemented by a spectacular increase in surveillance measures. The 122 to 189 censors appointed in Paris during the final four decades of French absolutism[65] repressed calumny and injurious speech, sometimes deploying a heavy

---

[61] J. Habermas, *The Structural Transformation of the Public Sphere: An Inquiry into a Category of Bourgeois Society*, (MIT Press, 1991), p. 30.

[62] I am summarizing observations I made in: P.-H. Monot, 'Poor, Nasty, British, and Short: Contemporary Pamphleteering, Popular Literacy, and the Politics of Literary Circulation', in M. Gamper, J. Müller-Tamm, D. Wachter, J. Wrobel, eds., *Der Wert der literarischen Zirkulation / The Value of Literary Circulation*, (Springer, 2023), pp. 173–185, 174.

[63] R. Darnton, *The Literary Underground of the Old Regime*, (Harvard University Press, 1982), pp. 29–34.

[64] For a seminal discussion of this point see: O. Negt, A. Kluge, *Öffentlichkeit und Erfahrung. Zur Organisationsanalyse von bürgerlicher und proletarischer Öffentlichkeit*, (Suhrkamp, 1973).

[65] S. Burrows, 'French Censorship on the Eve of the Revolution', in N. Moore, ed., *Censorship and the Limits of the Literary: A Global View*, (Bloomsbury, 2017), pp. 13–32, 14.

apparatus to identify and prosecute authors, printers, and readers alike. Robert Darnton has deftly outlined the exemplary case of an anti-monarchical poem that circulated under Louis XV:

> The poem crossed paths with five other poems, each of them seditious (at least in the eyes of the police) and each with its own diffusion pattern. They were copied on scraps of paper, traded for similar scraps, dictated to more copyists, memorized, declaimed, printed in underground tracts, adapted in some cases to popular tunes, and sung ... In the end, the police filled the Bastille with fourteen purveyors of poetry ... But they never found the author of the original verse. In fact, it may not have had an author, because people added and subtracted stanzas and modified phrasing as they pleased. It was a case of collective creation; and the first poem overlapped and intersected with so many others that, taken together, they created a field of poetic impulses, bouncing from one transmission point to another and filling the air with what the police called 'mauvais propos' or 'mauvais discours', a cacophony of sedition set to rhyme.[66]

In this way, the affordances of the pamphlet as an infrastructure of dissent contributed to standardizing the kind of information the police sought to obtain concerning authors: who had penned which libellous text? How did the text circulate? By whom, when, and where was it read? What were its political implications? In turn, pamphleteering and its surveillance helped consolidate a *legal* understanding of literary authorship (see Section 4), while granting booksellers and publishers comparative leniency and, more often than not, immunizing them from legal prosecution.[67] Hence, both socio-historical aspects are true at the same time: the Habermasian 'public

---

[66] R. Darnton, *Poetry and the Police: Communication Networks in Eighteenth-Century Paris*, (Belknap, 2010), p. 11.

[67] P. O. John, *Publishing in Paris, 1570–1590: A Bibliometric Analysis*, (Ph.D., University of St Andrews, 2010), pp. 22–31.

sphere' emerged in a context of not only secure deliberative institutions for the bourgeoisie, but also draconian policing measures against popular readerships. As I will point out in Sections 5 and 6, the policing, censorship, and control of licentious texts evolved hand in hand with sweeping infrastructural and political changes, ranging from desegregation in the United States to the generalization of internet access from the early 1990s onwards.

An extreme – and particularly famous – example of the practical interpenetration of legal containment and political provocation is nested as a fictional pamphlet in one of the Marquis de Sade's most brutal texts. De Sade had been sentenced to prison in 1790 for associating with counter-revolutionaries and on the charge, of all things, of 'moderatism'. Upon his release in 1793, he published *Philosophy in the Boudoir* (1795), which contains the mock pamphlet *Yet Another Effort, Frenchmen, if You Would Become Republicans*. Read aloud during the sexual education of fifteen-year-old Eugénie, the fictional pamphlet formulates atheistic propositions (God is 'an idea without object'[68]), argues that revolutionaries must transform the burgeoning Republic into a post-religious and fundamentally *amoral* one, and promotes '*prostitution, incest, rape*, and *sodomy*' as essential Republican activities. The Republic cannot preserve itself by moral means, the pamphlet concludes, 'for the republic will preserve itself only by war, and nothing is less moral than war. I ask how one will be able to demonstrate that in a state rendered immoral by its obligations, it is essential that the individual be moral? I will go further: it is a very good thing he is not'.[69]

De Sade stages the entire infrastructural imaginary of revolutionary pamphleteering. The pamphlet is 'bought outside the Palace of Equality ... straight from the press',[70] thereby locating polemical literature on the margins of the literary market and its mediating institutions (publishers, booksellers, censors). Its precepts are put into use, both sexually and politically, by its fictional readers, thereby pointing out that print polemic eschews the strictly interpretative or deliberative textual practices of the

---

[68] Marquis de Sade, *Philosophy in the Bedroom*, in R. Seaver, A. Wainhouse, eds., *Justine, Philosophy in the Bedroom, and Other Writings*, (Grove Press, 1965), pp. 179–367, p. 304.

[69] *Ibid.*, p. 314. [70] *Ibid.*, p. 309.

bourgeois public sphere. The comments of Sade's protagonists are further amalgamated with the primary text into precisely the kind of 'cacophony of sedition' described by Darnton, emphasizing the fact that pamphleteering is not a monological speech act, but a collective social practice. Finally, the pamphlet leads to the radical political transformation of Eugénie and the vindication of the most *outré* of libertine positions. This, then, is what every novelist and *romancier* could know about pamphleteering in the Revolutionary era: pamphleteering, once subjected to state surveillance, makes literature observable if not as a sexual fact, then at least as a social one.[71]

3.3 Ordinary Readers

What do we mean when we say that pamphlets address 'the people'? What kind of political body comes into being by virtue of being addressed by polemical texts in particular, rather than by literature or political speech in general? Few questions pertaining to the pamphlet have generated as many misunderstandings as this one. On the one hand, a 'culture of controversy'[72] did emerge among the broader reading public in the course of the sixteenth century, enabling a growing percentage of the population to engage in political and polemical disputes. On the other, however, the very *fragmentation* of readerships into distinct publics through polemical writing seems to belie the generality and inclusiveness implied by the pamphlet as a 'popular' practice.

Contrasting with Habermas's emphasis on social settings and institutions (salons, libraries, coffee houses, etc.), theorists attuned to the primarily democratic, rather than bourgeois, origins of the public sphere have emphasized readerly abilities as a condition of participation in political debates. Here, abilities that are distributed unequally among individuals

---

[71] I am summarizing: P.-H. Monot, 'Pretty Pamphlets', in P.-H. Monot, D. Bebnowski, S. Gröppmaier, eds., *Activist Writing: History, Politics, Rhetoric*, (Intercom, 2024), pp. 68–82.

[72] A. J. E. Deicke, 'Networks of Conflict: Analyzing the "Culture of Controversy" in Polemical Pamphlets of Intra-Protestant Disputes (1548–1580)', *Journal of Historical Network Research*, vol. 1 (2017), pp. 71–105, 72.

and social groups enable readerships to come into being and exercise their political agency. For Albert O. Hirschmann (literacy as the kind of 'persuadable temper'[73] conducive to agency), for a large segment of the African American literary tradition (literacy as freedom and agency[74]), and for recent waves in the sociology of literature,[75] the public sphere exists by virtue of individuals and groups exercising their reading competencies.[76] In turn, the way individuals and groups exert their political agency remains dependent on the way they gained these competencies in the first place. The political power of popular readerships bears the mark of formative reading experiences, specific literary styles, and modalities of circulation: 'published claim provoked printed counterclaim, vindication, denial, or agreement ... The more controversial print there was, the more need there was to enter into print to engage with it'.[77]

Of Thomas Paine's numerous pamphletary writings published during the American Revolutionary War, *Common Sense* (1776) perhaps best illustrates this process. The text, which calls for a shift to armed conflict and secession from Great Britain, begins by outlining a collective, transnational subject (a universal 'mankind'). Soon, however, Paine operates his own kind of textual secession, invoking a much more limited political body, a Republican We that must henceforth be distinguished from its continental

---

[73] A. O. Hirschman, 'Opinionated Opinions and Democracy', in J. Adelman, ed., *The Essential Hirschman*, (Princeton University Press, 2013), pp. 284–292, 289.

[74] D. E. McDowell, 'Telling Slavery in "Freedom's" Time: Post-reconstruction and the Harlem Renaissance', in A. Fisch, ed., *The Cambridge Companion to the African American Slave Narrative*, (Cambridge University Press, 2007), pp. 150–167.

[75] M. A. Thumala Olave, ed., *The Cultural Sociology of Reading: The Meanings of Reading and Books across the World*, (Palgrave Macmillan, 2022).

[76] P.-H. Monot, 'Poor, Nasty, British, and Short. Contemporary Pamphleteering, Popular Literacy, and the Politics of Literary Circulation', in M. Gamper, J. Müller-Tamm, D. Wachter, J. Wrobel, eds., *Der Wert der literarischen Zirkulation / The Value of Literary Circulation*, (Springer, 2023), pp. 173–185, 174–175.

[77] M. Knights, *Representation and Misrepresentation in Later Stuart Britain: Partisanship and Political Culture*, (Oxford University Press, 2006), p. 235.

counterpart[78] and to which Paine claims to have unmediated access precisely because it is a performative object: Paine's reading counterpublic is a 'kind of social totality' that merely 'exists by virtue of being addressed' (Michael Warner).[79] In fact, by the 1770s, literacy rates in the American colonies were exceptionally high, with a large percentage of white males having at least some degree of literacy, although exact numbers are disputed.[80] As a result, Paine's *Common Sense* circulated particularly well (Paine's own gross exaggerations notwithstanding, perhaps as many as 100,000 copies sold within the first year[81]).

Revolutionary pamphleteering therefore engaged in the twin pursuits of nation-building and cultivating an American knowledge industry[82] that would be attuned to the needs of a discontented readership: a readership that was widely scattered across the territories, that sometimes straddled milieus and social classes, and that was soon to enact a bloody partition of the body politic and declare its independence from Britain. In other words, these readerships differed fundamentally from the near-mythical *common readers* variously invoked by Samuel Johnson, Virginia Woolf, and the back covers of Penguin paperbacks in so far as they involved a logic of social decomposition and polarization, rather than of disinterested aesthetic

---

[78] T. Paine, 'Common Sense', in J. M. Opal, ed., *Common Sense and Other Writings*, (Norton, 2012), pp. 3–38, 33.

[79] M. Warner, *Publics and Counterpublics*, (Zone Books, 2002), p. 50. I am summarizing a longer essay on this question: P.-H. Monot, 'Pretty Pamphlets', in P.-H. Monot, D. Bebnowski, S. Gröppmaier, eds., *Activist Writing: History, Politics, Rhetoric*, (Intercom, 2024), pp. 68–82, p. 73.

[80] E. J. Monaghan, *Learning to Read and Write in Colonial America*, (University of Massachusetts Press, 2005), as well as: K. A. Lockridge. *Literacy in Colonial New England: An Enquiry into the Social Context of Literacy in the Early Modern West*, (Norton, 1974).

[81] G. S. Wood, *The American Revolution: A History*, (Modern Library, 2002), p. 80. T. Loughran, *The Republic in Print: Print Culture in the Age of U.S. Nation Building, 1770–1870*, (Columbia University Press, 2007), pp. 35–57.

[82] E. L. Eisenstein, *Divine Art, Infernal Machine: The Reception of Printing in the West from First Impressions to the Sense of an Ending*, (University of Pennsylvania Press, 2011), p. 63.

pursuits and learned inquiry. Paine's *Common Sense* had an impact on society precisely because it divided its readership into partisans and opponents: the pamphlet failed to find aesthetic and political commonality (i.e., a Johnsonian 'mirror in every mind') on account of its negation of political and aesthetic commonality from the outset.

Pamphletary readerships, at once historically contingent upon and rhetorically performed by polemical texts, are thus best thought of as *ordinary readers*. They are ordinary as much in the etymological sense of having authority to deal with political orders or norms directly rather than by deputation, as in the sense of always relating their readerly dispositions to their ordinary, daily, and concrete political circumstances. Ordinary readers use polemical literature *socially*: they read to effect normative changes, they discuss pamphlets to correct perceptions of their contingent political situation, and they circulate polemical literature to demand rights.[83] Paine himself expects no less of his readers, emphasizing the fundamental difference between common literary production and his own pamphletary works. While the former was necessarily 'ineffectual', Paine's revolutionary pamphlet adroitly manipulated the fears and aspirations of his literary constituency, demanding it divest itself of all its political attachments *and* literary habits.[84] Equating *Common Sense* with a sweeping 'act of oblivion', Paine originated the crucial rhetorical conceit of nineteenth- and twentieth-century polemical writing: pamphleteering was to secede from the bourgeois public sphere and demand that its uses be practical rather than symbolic. For Paine, as much as for his literary successors, 'the period of debate' must henceforth be considered 'closed'.[85]

---

[83] See also: R. A. Eberly, *Citizen Critics: Literary Public Spheres*, (University of Illinois Press, 2000), pp. 9–30.

[84] R. A. Ferguson, *Reading the Early Republic*, (Harvard University Press, 2004), p. 108.

[85] All quotes from Paine in this paragraph: T. Paine, 'Common Sense', in J. M. Opal, ed., *Common Sense and Other Writings*, (Norton, 2012), pp. 3–38, p. 16, 33.

4 Beneath the Public Sphere: Radical Pamphleteering 1898–1950

4.1 Ordinary Readers and Intellectuals

A new figure emerges at the dawn of the twentieth century: the 'intellectual', a term first used in the context of Émile Zola's *J'Accuse … !* (1898), and the Dreyfusard movement.[86] The *Affaire Dreyfus* revolved around the trial of Alfred Dreyfus, a French officer of Jewish ancestry. Convicted of treason and sentenced to life in 1895, Dreyfus maintained his innocence throughout the court proceedings. Zola's *J'Accuse … !*, arguably the most famous of all nineteenth-century pamphlets, was but one element in a vast movement that sought to exonerate Dreyfus.

'Intellectuals' – or *'les intellectuels'* – was initially used as a derogatory term against the French writers, politicians, artists, and journalists who sided with Dreyfus. The term implied a contestation of the political detachment often engendered by the hard-won artistic autonomy gained during the mid nineteenth century. Where *'auteurs'*, *'écrivains'*, and *'essayistes'* remained dependent on the limited legitimacy they had gained *as* authors, writers, or essayists, the intellectuals of the *Fin de Siècle* imposed a different social compact, now refusing to pay the price of literary autonomy with political quietism. Zola, then a best-selling novelist, reinvested his fame and legitimacy in an unprecedented act of political radicalism. By doing so, he not only redefined the social role of literature, he also retroactively asserted the moral and political integrity of his previous novelistic oeuvre. Zola's *J'Accuse … !* made 'acts of prophetic denunciation'[87] at once possible, profitable, and necessary for authorial self-positioning.[88] After close to a century of relative Romantic insularity, the

---

[86] D. Drake, *French Intellectuals and Politics from the Dreyfus Affair to the Occupation*, (Palgrave Macmillan, 2005), p. 8–34.

[87] P. Bourdieu, *The Rules of Art: Genesis and Structure of the Literary Field*, (Stanford University Press, 1995), p. 258.

[88] In this subsection, I am summarizing arguments I have developed in much greater detail in: P.-H. Monot, 'Poor, Nasty, Brutish, and Short: Contemporary Technological Pamphleteering, Popular Literacy, and the Politics of Literary

turn of the twentieth century saw the emergence of a pamphletary market that was increasingly indistinguishable from the rest of the literary industry. Pamphleteering, in short, gained legitimacy both as a literary exercise and as an activity for novelists.

Yet turn-of-the-century pamphleteering was also a continuation of the strategies that had marked polemical literature since the French and American revolutions. The distinction between practical and symbolic uses of literature, perhaps most clearly contrasted in Paine's *Common Sense*, became an object of incessant criticism, sometimes precipitating criminalization, prosecution and, in Zola's case, banishment. Zola's seminal innovation in *J'Accuse . . . !* was arguably his particularly insightful critique of the limits of 'literature' as a social institution. Its historical attachment to the clear demarcation of practical from symbolic uses of language, its habitual political lethargy, its tendency to side with affluent social classes and to abuse religious minorities were the object of all of Zola's numerous *Dreyfusard* writings. Yet Zola brought his detractors to a boil by flaunting the legal implications of his last pamphlet: 'In making these accusations I am aware that I am making myself liable to articles 30 and 31 of the July 29, 1881 law on the press making libel a punishable offense. I expose myself to that risk voluntarily . . . I am waiting'.[89]

By naming names, by calling for legal consequences, by defaming members of the public, Zola forced the bourgeois public sphere of the Third Republic to react in ways it usually considered to be incompatible with higher aesthetic, political, and moral pursuits. In order to respond to the accusations levelled in *J'Accuse . . . !*, the French literary field had to

---

Circulation', in M. Gamper, J. Müller-Tamm, D. Wachter, J. Wrobel, eds., *Der Wert der literarischen Zirkulation / The Value of Literary Circulation*, (Metzler, 2022), pp. 173–185, as well as: P.-H. Monot, 'Kill Lists: Ideas of Order in the Pamphlet', *KWI Blog*, (20 April 2022), https://doi.org/10.37189/kwi-blog/20220420-0830.

[89] P.-H. Monot, 'Émile Zola: "J'accuse . . . !": A Commented Bilingual Edition, Including Contextual Sources and a Facsimile Copy of Émile Zola's Manuscript', in P.-H. Monot, ed., *The Arts of Autonomy: A Living Anthology of Polemical Literature*, (The Arts of Autonomy, 2022), pp. 8–9.

acknowledge that its own verbal rituals had direct material effects on the existence and livelihood of its opponents. Hence, *J'Accuse . . . !* pointed out that 'literature' and its institutions were but nominally independent from the bourgeoisie. By doing so, Zola put pamphleteering and 'literature' on an equal footing. Writing 'literature' in general, rather than just pamphlets in particular, had to be understood as a fully *political* action. In the months that followed, Zola was convicted of criminal libel, barely six months before Major Hubert Joseph Henry confessed to having forged documents brought forward in the trial against Dreyfus.[90]

4.2 A Polemical Education

Pamphleteering was now invested with a crucial function: it tested and expanded the social power of literature and its sanctioned institutions. From the *Affaire* to the beginning of WWII, the term 'public intellectual' gained in popularity and soon became a staple of journalistic discourse. It was also a near-pleonasm: to be an 'intellectual' meant exercising one's rationality publicly. The public reinvestment of one's notoriety in favour of a political cause was soon perceived to be the crucial gesture reading publics could demand from their *intellectuels*.[91]

In turn, the slow democratization of free, mandatory, and secular education (the 'Jules Ferry Laws' of 1881 and 1882) not only helped secularize the Republic, it also soon produced a mass readership that was well versed in the rudiments of literary history, geography, political economy, law, and the natural sciences.[92] The infrastructure of the publishing industry adapted to a growing popular readership, launching successive series of paperbound books (Tauchnitz in 1841, Reclam in 1867), affordable hardback formats (Everyman's Library in 1906, Nelson in 1910, Calmann-Lévy in 1938) and, later yet, mass-market paperback editions (Albatross

---

[90] Here I am condensing arguments I have developed in much greater detail in: *Ibid*, pp. 3–11.

[91] *Ibid*.

[92] A. M. Chartier, *L'école et la lecture obligatoire: Histoire et paradoxes des pratiques d'enseignement de la lecture*, (Retz, 2015).

Books in 1932, Penguin in 1935, Simon & Schuster in 1939, Éditions du Seuil in 1951).[93]

Yet by the same token, the distinction between mass-market publishing and the infrastructure of print polemic became increasingly fuzzy. On the one hand, the distinction remained intact: the radical pamphlets of the early twentieth century did not circulate among reading publics the same way canonical or pedagogical literature did. Open letters, manifestos, and radical pamphlets were published in the daily press, in small, private, and sometimes pirate editions, or via party or gallery imprints – but rarely by the same publishers who supplied mandatory education with pedagogical treatises and literary raw material. On the other hand, however, some publishers viewed the serial formats of the nineteenth century as an opportunity to blur the fine line separating serialized fiction from short-form polemic.[94] Publishers like Jules Rouff laboured the point: if Hugo's *Les Misérables* could be reprinted in weekly instalments at 10 *centimes* for a general readership, so could a much more radical *Socialist History 1789–1900*, edited by Rouff's friend Jean Jaurès and serialized for half the price (see Figure 4).[95] In turn, Jaurès himself experimented with the transformation of the publishing industry: his ferocious press articles written in support of Capitaine Dreyfus and calling for a retrial were soon collected in book form and circulated as radical polemical literature, rather than as journalistic ephemera. Authors and publishers now perceived polemical texts to be both more profitable and more respectable than they had been throughout the nineteenth century. A general loosening of established markets and literary taxonomies soon took hold of the industry. Why, after all, should short-form polemical literature be understood to be a greater threat than the

---

[93] A. McCleery, 'The Paperback Evolution: Tauchnitz, Albatross and Penguin', in N. Matthews, N. Moody, eds., *Judging a Book By its Cover: Fans, Publishers, Designers and the Marketing of Fiction*, (Ashgate, 2007), pp. 3–18.

[94] N. Cetre, *L'édition en fascicules de romans français entre 1870 et 1914 et leur conservation par la BnF*, (Ecole Nationale Supérieure des Sciences de l'Information et des Bibliothèques, 2002).

[95] S. Basart, *Les Éditions Jules Rouff (1877–1912): Monographie d'un éditeur populaire*, (Université de Saint Quentin en Yvelines, 1994).

Figure 4 Jules Chéret, poster for Jules Rouff's serialized edition of Victor Hugo's *Les Misérables*, 1886. Source: gallica.bnf.fr / Bibliothèque nationale de France.

socialist or anarchist tropes that were now staples in literary fiction? By the mid twentieth century, across the Seine, publisher Jean-Jacques Pauvert would simultaneously publish Hugo's complete novels and, for the first time, the unexpurgated *Works* of the Marquis de Sade, including the mock pamphlet *Yet Another Effort, Frenchmen, if You Would Become Republicans*.

If the distinction between pamphleteering and literature could now be productively and profitably undermined by authors and publishers alike, this general shift was flanked by a series of even more consequential social-historical tensions. In France, mandatory education had brought about a distinct social type in the form of the *Hussards noirs* ('Black Hussars', so named for their frightful black coats and black caps). These schoolteachers, who usually had provincial origins and scarce economic resources, were often perceived as the Republican elite precisely because Republicanism constituted the core of their pedagogical goals. Their radical attachment to Republican virtues and their staunch anti-clerical ethos not only instilled defiance towards the Church in their overwhelmingly Catholic pupils, but also contributed to normalizing ad personam attacks and rhetorical excesses as legitimate modes of argumentation in civil society. The supreme values of the Republic (in Zola's own pamphlet: 'humanity', 'truth', and 'justice'), the widely shared belief in what Catholic-nationalist polemicist Charles Péguy derided as the 'positivist metaphysics'[96] of progress, the rapid urbanization of the population, steady increases in life expectancy, the allocation of leisure time, a liberal legislation on free speech and censorship, and spectacular increases in literacy rates all contributed to the social acceptance of open conflict in writing. Hence, by 1913, Péguy could publish the sober promise to 'shoot Jaurès'[97] without fearing censorship (Jaurès was, in fact, shot by a nationalist one year later). That same year, other pamphleteers resorted to publicizing the sadomasochistic sexual mores of Prime Minister Louis Barthou (these accusations were by all accounts factual[98]). Here too, it was the invocation of Republican radicalism that served to legitimize the thematic continuity of revolutionary and turn-of-the-century pamphleteering, with both of them showcasing a strong interest in the genital peculiarities of monarchs and ministers alike. In 1798 as much as in 1913, few rhetorical tropes held as much weight as declaring one's ruler to be not only politically powerless, but also sexually impotent.

Yet this culture of personalized controversy simultaneously stood in stark contradiction to the avowed project of *democratizing* the expectations, habits, and moral proclivities of the bourgeoisie. This project was explicit in the foundational texts of the school reform movement of the 1870s onwards, which routinely bemoaned 'the absence of intercourse' between social milieus and 'a mutual uneasiness between the people and

---

[96] My translation. C. Péguy, *L'Argent*, (Gallimard, 1932), p. 31.

[97] My translation. G. Leroy, (2014), 'Je pars, soldat de la République', in G. Leroy, ed., *Charles Péguy: L'inclassable*, (Armand Colin, 2014), pp. 291–296.

[98] Generally: R. J. Young, *Power and Pleasure: Louis Barthou and the Third French Republic*, (McGill-Queen's University Press, 1991).

the bourgeoisie'.[99] Thus, the moderation of agonal conflict, the modulation of insults and calumny, and the tabooing of open discussions of sexual promiscuity were structural necessities: they ensured that commerce – both verbal and mercantile – could flourish across classes despite often opposing interests, social positions, and ambitions. In other words, pamphleteering always ran the risk of undermining the very political and behavioural '*civisme*' (understood both as polite civility and as civic sense) which had, albeit paradoxically, legitimized pamphleteering as a Republican form in the first place.

The highly ambiguous position of the pamphlet as both a Republican and a potentially socially destructive format was stabilized by its readership itself, as well as by its ingrained readerly dispositions. The emergence of what historians have described as a 'radical bourgeoisie' was decisive. Deeply Republican and attached to universal rights (in either their 1798 formulation as *Droits de l'homme* or their 1791 precedent as Paine's *Rights of Man* – the difference carries little weight here), the radical bourgeoisie was also engaged in a process of democratic nation-building begun in 1792 and interrupted during the Second French Empire (1852–1870).[100] The threat posed by polemic was resolved by simultaneously banishing excessive polemic from school materials *and* enabling pupils to participate in open polemic as *citoyens*, that is, as a specific type of bourgeois citizen that was encouraged to read, share, and discursively moderate radical polemical statements. While diatribe and the most radical pamphletary styles would henceforth be banished from schools, mandatory education would simultaneously enable citizens to polemicize as Republican citizens, thereby placing great pedagogical and political importance on literacy and abstract discursive principles. This perhaps best explains two immediate consequences of Zola's *J'Accuse . . . !*.

---

[99] J. Macé in 1867, quoted after: K. Auspitz, *The Radical Bourgeoisie: The Ligue de l'Enseignement Supérieur and the origins of the Third Republic, 1866–1885*, (Cambridge University Press, 2002), p. 90.

[100] K. Auspitz, *The Radical Bourgeoisie: The Ligue de l'Enseignement Supérieur and the origins of the Third Republic, 1866–1885*, (Cambridge University Press, 2002), pp. 4–10.

The first is social: intellectuals now had the support of the radical bourgeoisie and increasingly acted as mediators between reading publics, pamphleteers, state institutions, and the bourgeoisie itself. In fact, the countless answers and rejoinders prompted by the publication of *J'Accuse … !* drew much of their weight from the institutional affiliation of their authors, who soon came to be known as the '*maîtres de la Sorbonne*' – academics of all stripes who could mobilize important symbolic resources for political causes. Hence, *J'Accuse … !* not only instigated the formation of a coalition of new social actors, it also suggested that scientific truth and political truth were cut from the same cloth.[101] If 'truth marches on', as Zola claimed in *J'Accuse … !*, it did so only because it was flanked by both scientific competences and the universal moral imperatives of justice, freedom, and *political* truth.[102]

The second consequence of the banishment of excessive polemic from schools and the simultaneous habituation of pupils to open polemical debate was a turn towards abstraction in turn-of-the-century pamphleteering. The extremely harsh penalties Zola incurred for *J'Accuse … !* served as a stern warning to polemical publics and led pamphleteers to fight on more general, less individualized, less specified terrain. Polemicizing for 'truth', 'justice', or 'equality', rather than attacking specific social actors or libelling individuals allowed pamphleteers to criticize the personnel and institutions of the Republic *in the name of its own values*. In so doing, Republican pamphleteering could now pose as a prototypical Republican activity that spared the sensibilities and respectability of notable figures. Readers could therefore be addressed directly in a bid to effect normative change with the full legitimacy conferred by Republican self-criticism.

---

[101] L. Dartigues, 'Une généalogie de *l'intellectuel spécifique*', *Astérion*, vol. 12, (2014), pp. 1–16.

[102] Here I am summarizing arguments I have developed in greater detail in: P.-H. Monot, 'Émile Zola: "J'accuse … !": A Commented Bilingual Edition, Including Contextual Sources and a Facsimile Copy of Émile Zola's Manuscript', in P.-H. Monot, ed., *The Arts of Autonomy: A Living Anthology of Polemical Literature*, (The Arts of Autonomy, 2022), pp. 1–91.

4.3 Pamphleteering as Norm: The Artistic Avant-Gardes

In fact, while the scope and intensity of polemical accusations kept expanding until the outbreak of WWII, they generally remained within the confines of an outdated historical model: polemical literature often imitated *oral* communication in secluded social settings (in essence: the salon or the *Café*) and generally upheld its imperatives of relative decency and tact.[103] The obligation of sparing one's discursive opponent the humiliation of insult and verbal defeat in the presence of equals[104] became entrenched as a style, a political necessity, and a commercial logic in all European and American pamphletary markets.

The oral imaginary of pamphleteering nevertheless began to erode with the European Avant-Gardes of the late 1910s and 1920s. All defining artistic movements of the era not only turned to pamphleteering as a natural vector of publicity and expression, they also did so in a way that publicly signified a decisive break with the modes of communication that had marked pamphleteering from the Revolutions of the eighteenth century to the social transformations of the late nineteenth century.

On the one hand, they broke with the implicit orality of protest by experimenting with typography. The canonical pamphlets of the era all made use of the formal innovations of European and American Modernisms to unsettle pamphletary statements and disorganize dissent on the printed page. The innumerable manifestos, open letters, tracts, and leaflets of the various Dadaist groups scattered across Europe notably drew on the *Calligrammes* of poet Guillaume Apollinaire, published in 1918, as well as on the new visual languages of advertisement,[105] often using collages and visual puns to voice polemical claims (see Figure 5). Instead of ensuring the legibility of political demands by the greatest numbers of readers – a priority for the overwhelming majority of pamphleteers since the Reformation – Dada loudly emphasized its own 'ability to hypnotize',

---

[103] A. Kieserling, *Kommunikation unter Anwesenden: Studien über Interaktionssysteme*, (Suhrkamp, 1999), p. 441.

[104] N. Luhmann, *Social Systems*, (Stanford University Press, 1995), pp. 414–455.

[105] A. McStay, *Creativity and Advertising: Affect, Events and Process*, (Routledge, 2013), pp. 41–43.

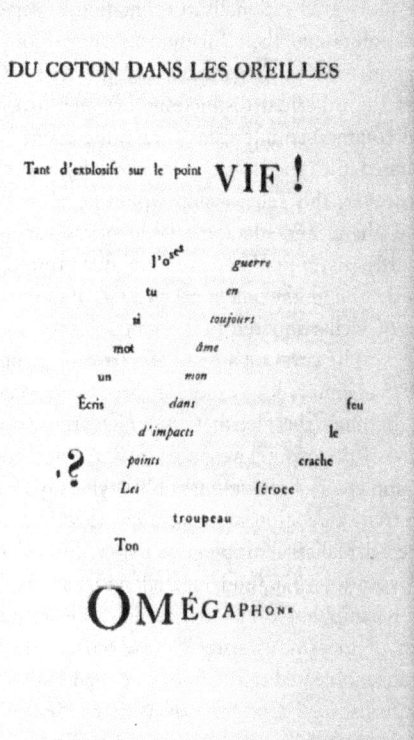

Figure 5 Guillaume Apollinaire, 'Ears Plugged', *Calligrammes: Poèmes de la guerre et de la paix, 1913–1916*. Source: gallica.bnf.fr / Bibliothèque nationale de France.

rather than its willingness to sway public opinion on rational grounds. Dada's calls for 'the introduction of progressive unemployment', the 'compulsory adherence of all clergymen and teachers to the Dadaist articles of faith', and the 'requisition of churches for the performance of bruitism'[106] were never motivated rationally. Ostentatiously rejecting both their discursive constraints and their function as vectors of 'public opinion', the staunchly antitheoretical[107] pamphlets of the Avant-Gardes blurred what remained of the inherited distinctions between artistic practice, political dissent, and commercial interests. In fact, the poetics of dissent sometimes closely imitated the poetics of commerce; by the end of the twentieth century, however, this relationship would be reversed, with dissent now providing aesthetic and ideological blueprints for a commercial culture geared towards 'disruption' and commodified protest.[108]

On the other hand, the polemical writings of the Avant-Gardes outpaced the rhythm of well-tempered oral communication in their sheer quantity and frequency. The constant stream of Surrealist pamphlets issued between 1924 and 1945 – sometimes as short as three lines, sometimes as long as 100 pages – highlighted the fact that pamphleteering could now lay claim to a large share of the group's resources. While eighteenth- and nineteenth-century pamphleteers and reading publics typically coalesced around single causes (a retrial, a taxation measure, the support of an identifiable constituency), the Surrealists multiplied occasions for polemical statements and obscene provocations that fundamentally violated the decorum of the public sphere: their pamphlets celebrated recent sadistic murders, called for the beatification of incestuous sisters, protested against the state funeral of Anatole France, objected to the Paris Colonial Exposition of 1931, derided the First International Congress of Writers for the Defence of Culture (1935) on account of its conformism and ineffectiveness, and relentlessly attacked individual creativity and its social rites (prizes, academies, the very notion of literature).[109]

---

[106] R. Huelsenbeck, *En Avant Dada*, in R. Motherwell, ed., *The Dada Painters and Poets: An Anthology*, (Harvard University Press, 1981), pp. 21–48, p. 31.

[107] P. Bürger, *Theory of the Avant-Garde*, (Manchester University Press, 1984), pp. 15–34.

[108] L. Boltanksi, E. Chiapello, *The New Spirit of Capitalism*, (Verso, 2007).

[109] B. Péret, *Je ne mange pas de ce pain-là*, (Syllepse, 2010).

Pamphleteering 39

The logic of scandal, 'the public event par excellence',[110] buttressed the radical insurgency *and* the economic interests of the Surrealist group to such a degree that one may rightly speak of an 'autonomization' of the pamphletary field. To put it another way, the sheer intensity of the polemical activity of the Surrealists (and this is true of all continental avant-gardes of the 1920s and 1930s) sometimes undermined the urgency of its political causes and occasionally contradicted the agency of polemical literature; the publication of a steady stream of invectives and denunciations could produce unwanted effects, obscuring pressing issues and famously alienating sympathizers and fellow 'travellers of the world revolution'[111] (notably the Dadaists and the French Communist Party, as well as several of the founding members of the Surrealist group itself[112]).

In effect, Pierre Bourdieu notes, 'the more one moves through history, that is, through the process of autonomization of the field, the more the manifestos ... tend to be reduced to pure manifestations of difference (though one should not draw the conclusion that they are inspired by the cynical search for distinction)'.[113] The Surrealists used the infrastructure of textual dissent developed by their predecessors to both pursue political goals and assume specified and desirable positions in the literary field of the Third French Republic. By the time the Surrealist movement was born in 1924, the legitimate social uses of the pamphlet had therefore diversified.

4.4 Pamphlets or Manifestos: Taxonomies of Dissent

At this stage, it is necessary to spell out (and dispel) an ambiguity that has marred most of the scholarship on nineteenth- and twentieth-century polemical literature. The term 'manifesto' is often used interchangeably with that of 'pamphlet'. While it is true that many of the most notorious

---

[110] A. Adut, *On Scandal: Moral Disturbances in Society, Politics, and Art*, (Cambridge University Press, 2009), p. 5.

[111] B. Studer, *Travellers of the World Revolution: A Global History of the Communist International*, (Verso, 2023).

[112] S. Baker, *Surrealism, History, and Revolution*, (Peter Lang, 2003), pp. 33–38.

[113] P. Bourdieu, *The Rules of Art: Genesis and Structure of the Literary Field*, (Stanford University Press, 1995), p. 240.

polemical texts of the era self-identified or were marketed as nominal 'manifestos', and while manifestos fully participate in the long tradition of pamphletary writing, this conflation has created a series of methodological problems and historical ambiguities for historians of literature and book historians alike.

While texts published as early as the sixteenth century had occasionally described themselves as manifestos (alongside other, more common generic denominators such as the *petition*, *call*, or *appeal*), the historical nexus of this ambiguity is perhaps most easily and fruitfully placed alongside the publication of Karl Marx and Friedrich Engels' *Manifesto of the Communist Party*. This most famous and influential of all manifestos is, for several reasons, perhaps also the least typical exponent of the genre. Since its publication in 1848, innumerable other texts have adopted the term in their very title: the *1979 Conservative Party General Election Manifesto* and its foreword by Margaret Thatcher, the *Futurist Manifesto* (1909), the *Secular Humanist Manifesto* (1980), the techno-utopian *Cluetrain Manifesto* (1999), and Valerie Solana's *SCUM Manifesto* (1967), to name but a few of the more familiar ones among a global archive of several thousands. In effect, the genre of the manifesto has crowded out other self-descriptions of polemical literature, while homogenizing an ever more diverse set of claims and styles. What, in fact, does the *SCUM Manifesto* have in common with the *Startup Manifesto*[114] or the *Superfood Manifesto* ('Don't eat a lot of candy'[115]), other than their generic self-description?

A fundamental – and methodologically interesting – asymmetry between both genres is often overlooked. While nominal manifestos constitute an ever-growing and lucrative archive, instances of polemical texts describing themselves as 'a pamphlet' are exceedingly rare. As a descriptor, the term 'pamphlet' is usually attributed by readers, censors, surveillance personnel, prosecutors, and literary historians, rather than by authors and

---

[114] Z. Dentzel, D. Ek, K. Hed, et al., *Startup Manifesto: A Manifesto for Entrepreneurship & Innovation to Power Growth in the EU*, www.startupmanifesto.eu/#manifesto.

[115] A. Castronovo, 'A Superfood Manifesto', *Blast Magazine*, 23 June 2011, https://blastmagazine.com/2011/06/23/a-superfood-manifesto/.

Pamphleteering 41

publishers. Conversely, the term 'manifesto' is used by authors and publishers to define and market a publication but is seldom used by readers and literary historians to describe texts that would not have the term 'manifesto' in their title. This is best explained not by the respective formal or ideological features of the manifesto and pamphlet, which are often indistinguishable, but by their starkly different social uses.

Let me briefly summarize some canonical scholarly positions on the manifesto to elucidate this genre and format. Scholars have tried to specify its ideological particularities, almost always taking Marx and Engels' seminal text as their formal starting point, if not their historical one. For Kenneth Burke, manifestos can be traced back to the logic of modern Constitutions, themselves 'Great Manifestos' of a kind, as well as to the process of declaring, instituting, and enacting rights and norms taken to be inalienable (the 'self-evident' truths of the US Declaration of Independence, for instance). Manifestos are inherently pragmatic in the sense that they outline not only a series of inalienable norms ('Life, Liberty and the pursuit of Happiness', 'Liberté, Égalité, Fraternité', etc.), but also the historical and political measures necessary to obtain and defend them: 'in the Manifesto's closing challenge, we see what 'views and aims' may do, not simply as reflecting conditions, but as guides for the changing of conditions'.[116]

For Hayden White, manifestos are the genre most conducive to an ironic emplotment of historical narrative. Because manifestos simultaneously describe objective social conditions in the present *and* desirable aims in the future, they allow their author to 'claim the title of a 'realist' while sustaining his dream of a Utopian reconciliation of man with man *beyond* the social state'.[117] As such, the manifesto is the main literary vector by which utopias may acquire plausibility for readerships.

Conversely, Marjorie Perloff argues that the manifestos of the early twentieth century announced the end of the political field as a strictly distinct and clearly outlined realm in the distribution of power in modern societies. The manifesto's inherent hybridity allowed otherwise marginal

---

[116] K. Burke, *A Grammar of Motives*, (Prentice-Hall, 1945), p. 207, 340.
[117] H. White, *Metahistory: The Historical Imagination in Nineteenth-Century Europe*, (Johns Hopkins University Press, 2014), p. 310.

social actors to transform 'what had traditionally been a vehicle for political statement into a literary, one might say, a quasi-poetic construct'.[118] Doing so, they introduced 'propaganda' as the default mode of political participation for the artists and writers of the European Avant-Gardes.

Finally, Martin Puchner emphasizes the performative aspect of political and artistic manifestos. Here, manifestos are speech acts that are 'singularly invested in doing things with words, in changing the world'. Puchner suggests that the roots of this performative power lie in a dual historical lineage. On the one hand, the '*Manifeste*' (German, plural) of sovereign communication were 'authored by those in authority, by the state, the military, or the church'. They were grounded in an authority that was both undisputed and, more importantly, that did not depend on being communicated in the first place: *Manifeste* manifested an existing power. On the other hand, however, the religious figure of revelation or manifestation (the burning bush, the son, or Scripture) provided manifestos with the kind of ambiguity necessary for utopian political work. In manifestos and religious manifestations alike, nascent aims, new desires, and desirable norms were 'revealed' to the audience. Yet they had 'uncertain results and effects', unlike speech acts performed by and with authority: the realization of political and religious 'manifestation' remained dependent on interpretation and was therefore necessarily 'laborious and prone to failure'. Puchner concludes that whenever a manifesto 'turns against the state and its authority, it appeals precisely to this alternate authority of religious revelation'.[119]

All these definitions also apply to the majority of pamphletary literature, as well as to many more marginal examples of polemical communication. Yet what these definitions of the manifesto also have in common is that they minimize the importance of the social existence of polemical literature (see Figure 6). In fact, they all dispense with considering the role of reading publics, printing infrastructures, and circulation networks in not only the elaboration

---

[118] M. Perloff, *The Futurist Moment: Avant-Garde, Avant Guerre, and the Language of Rupture*, (University of Chicago Press, 1982), pp. 82–83.

[119] M. Puchner, *Poetry of the Revolution: Marx, Manifestos, and the Avant-Gardes*, (Princeton University Press, 2006), pp. 12–13.

Night Gathering of Tramps, Printers and "Pan Jerkers" on the Battery, New York City.

Figure 6 'Night Gathering of Tramps, Printers, and 'Pan Jerkers' on the Battery, New York City'. Allan Pinkerton, *Strikers, Communists, Tramps and Detectives*. New York, G. W. Carleton & Co, 1878. Library of Congress.

and circulation, but more importantly the reception and effectuation of polemical claims. The power of reading publics to identify and circulate polemical texts deemed worthy of attention or conducive to political change is treated, at best, like an epiphenomenon of specific literary styles.

It is remarkable, by contrast, that scholars of the pamphlet proper almost always emphasize the place of publics in the making of the genre, sometimes going as far as to propose sweeping definitions from the perspective of a fictive historical reader: 'For such a reader the interconnections between the material, the commercial, the literary and the political in forming the pamphlet, in making it work as a means of speaking out, informing, and cultivating public opinion, would probably have been obvious'.[120] For

---

[120] J. Raymond, *Pamphlets and Pamphleteering in Early Modern Britain*, (Cambridge University Press, 2003), p. 383.

George Orwell, the pamphlet is best defined by its self-evidence and from the perspective of its presumptive reader:

> To ask 'What is a pamphlet?' is rather like asking 'What is a dog?' We all know a dog when we see one, or at least we think we do, but it is not easy to give a clear verbal definition, not even to distinguish at sight between a dog and some kindred creature such as a wolf or a jackal.[121]

Orwell emphasizes two of its distinct features: a pamphlet is inexpensive and written for 'a large public'.[122] The bulk of recent scholarship on pamphlets has emphasized this point and highlighted 'unrestricted discursive opportunity'[123] presented by pamphlets whenever they successfully trigger large-scale discussions of their claims. Hence, scholarship has tacitly conferred to reading publics the signal legitimacy of identifying, and thus 'making' pamphlets, regardless of their formal makeup, text length, and generic self-description. To put it another way, the apparent truism according to which 'the historical significance of the pamphlets lies in the fact that they were read and thereby exercised social influence'[124] must be granted full attention.

It is indeed significant that one of the early foundational definitions of Book History as an academic discipline was formulated by a scholar of Revolutionary pamphleteering. Robert Darnton's frequently cited essay

---

[121] G. Orwell, 'Introduction', G. Orwell, R. Reynolds, eds., *British Pamphleteers. Volume 1, From the Sixteenth Century to the French Revolution*, (Allan Wingate, 1948), pp. 7–17, p. 7.

[122] *Ibid.*, p. 7. S. Gröppmaier, *Textualizing Upheaval: The Pamphletary Politics of Secessionist Movements in the Digital Public Sphere*, (Dissertation, Ludwig-Maximilians-Universität München, 2024), pp. 28–29.

[123] A. Halasz, *The Marketplace of Print: Pamphlets and the Public Sphere in Early Modern England*, (Cambridge University Press, 1997), p. 14.

[124] J. Raymond, *Pamphlets and Pamphleteering in Early Modern Britain*, (Cambridge University Press, 2003), p. 26. See also: M. Winter, *Finance, Commerce, and Politics in Seventeenth-Century England: The Case of Thompson and Company 1671–1678*, (University of Sheffield, 2020), p. 30.

delves into the 'life cycle' of books as the appropriate ontology for (and methodological innovation of) Book History. This cycle

> could be described as a communications circuit that runs from the author to the publisher (if the bookseller does not assume that role), the printer, the shipper, the bookseller, and the reader. The reader completes the circuit, because he influences the author both before and after the act of composition. Authors are readers themselves. By reading and associating with other readers and writers, they form notions of genre and style and a general sense of the literary enterprise ... Book history concerns each phase of this process and the process as a whole, in all its variations over space and time and in all its relations with other systems.[125]

Robert Darnton's emphasis on the 'life cycle' of books and on the way they 'spread through society' would, in fact, seem to apply to a minority of books only, while also excluding pre-print manuscripts. Yet Darnton's model does apply to most pamphlets. To rephrase, I want to suggest that the pamphlet is perhaps best understood as the *epistemic unconscious* of the early years of Book History: the social life of books, or what was then known as 'the sociology of texts',[126] was routinely extrapolated from both the highly specific modalities of pamphletary circulation and the way publics identified or 'made' pamphletary claims worthy of circulation, reproduction, discussion, and enactment. The sustained criticism of Darnton's approach admittedly belongs to the annals of the discipline itself.[127] Yet the universalization of the pamphlet as the paradigmatic 'book' in early Book History, as well as the generalization of a highly

---

[125] R. Darnton, 'What is the History of Books?', *Daedalus* 111(3), pp. 65–83, 67.

[126] D. F. McKenzie, *Bibliography and the Sociology of Texts*, (Cambridge University Press, 2004).

[127] See for instance: T. R. Adams, N. Barker, 'A New Model for the Study of the Book', in N. Barker, ed., *A Potencie of Life: Books in Society. The Clark Lectures 1986–1987*, (The British Library, 1993), pp. 5–43.

particular case of the 'socialization of texts'[128] remain symptomatic of the ambiguity attached to polemical literature in general, and to the pamphlet in particular.

As a simplification of what remains a contentious taxonomical debate, I would emphasize three relatively uncomplicated distinctions that help specify the pamphlet and distinguish it from cognate genres such as the manifesto, although they often overlap.

First, the historical pamphlets at the disposal of historians are usually those that circulated successfully. The attribution of the generic term 'pamphlet' is often retrospective and dependent on a reading public's demonstrated recognition of the import of a given polemical text. Manifestos, on the other hand, frequently fail to elicit significant public interest. As such, Marx and Engels' *Manifesto of the Communist Party* is perhaps best thought of as a generic exception: while it was a nominal manifesto, it was also a 'pamphlet' on account both of its mass circulation and the import attributed to it by successive reading publics around the globe (see Figure 7).[129] By contrast, the *Superfood Manifesto* should not be considered a pamphlet, despite its brevity and rhetorical gesturing towards radical literature. In short: pamphlets are polemical texts that circulate well and do so because of the popular interest and support they elicit.

Second, texts retrospectively considered to be or to have been pamphlets almost always responded to great social stresses.[130] They were often embedded in extant social tensions or debates and, in turn, triggered a set of typical responses from the public, ranging from orderly public discussions to popular riots. Pamphleteering is a collective activity that societies turn to in highly contentious historical circumstances for lack of strategic or medial alternatives. Pamphlets are a medium of last (or only) resort.

---

[128] J. McGann, *The Textual Condition*, (Princeton University Press, 1991), pp. 69–87.

[129] S. Kremmel, 'Born Translated Manifesto', in P.-H. Monot, D. Bebnowski, S. Gröppmaier, eds., *Activist Writing: History, Politics, Rhetoric*, (Intercom, 2024), pp. 98–111.

[130] M. Galchinsky, 'Political Pamphlet', in F. Burwick, ed., *The Encyclopedia of Romantic Literature*, Vol. 2, (Wiley-Blackwell, 2012), pp. 1025–1034, 1025.

Karl Marx en Prométhée, lithographie anonyme 1843

Figure 7 Anonymous, 'Karl Marx as Prometheus', *L'art dans la révolution bourgeoise*, 1843. CC0 Paris Musées / Musée Carnavalet – Histoire de Paris

Conversely, manifestos usually are not and often dispense with engaging explicitly and violently with an identified sociopolitical context or normative horizon.

Third, most pamphlets are 'rubbish', a fact which must have been 'true at all times',[131] as Orwell observed. They often, if not always, dispense with

---

[131] G. Orwell, 'Introduction', G. Orwell, R. Reynolds, eds., *British Pamphleteers: Volume 1, From the Sixteenth Century to the French Revolution*, (London: Allan Wingate, 1948), pp. 7–17, p. 13.

elaborate rhetorical and aesthetic strategies and instead emphasize clarity and directness in addressing extant normative orders. They are akin to *life* itself, if only in the Hobbesian sense of the term: poor, nasty, brutish, and short. Pamphlets are media of diminishing opportunities and growing demands: they must thereby bear the brunt of unfulfilled aspirations without recourse to organized, aestheticized, and recognized forms of political agency. In contrast to the pamphlet, manifestos are often but a component of larger-scale political, artistic, or commercial enterprises. Manifestos, therefore, usually add little more than a textual surplus to aspirations buttressed by other political, artistic, or commercial means. As such, they must often meet the standards and match the interests of systemic gatekeepers.[132] In short, manifestos are almost always *literary* reconfigurations of other political vectors, and almost always necessarily so; pamphlets seldom are.

In the following section, however, I want to argue that these distinctions, while they clarify important aspects of the literatures and social modalities of dissent, also invite us to adopt a different attitude towards polemical literature altogether. Robert Darnton's much criticized exposition of the 'life cycle' of books, for all its imprecisions as a paradigm in Book History, does in fact provide the opportunity to conceive of pamphleteering as a collective activity that radically shifts the focus from immanent textual considerations to social practices.

---

[132] See the introduction to: W. Marling, *Gatekeepers: The Emergence of World Literature & the 1960s*, (Oxford University Press, 2016), pp. 1–11.

5 The Civil Rights Movement: A Pamphletary Event

5.1 Booms, Waves, Clusters

Social historians and historians of polemical literature have often noted that polemical literature comes and goes in 'booms', 'clusters', 'waves', and other assorted metaphors. The political implications and methodological approaches differ in each case, even though all draw attention to the fact that the production of pamphletary literature varies much more significantly across decades than it does for other literary genres, styles, and formats. The various pamphletary 'booms'[133] of the eighteenth, mid nineteenth, early twentieth, and mid twentieth centuries, for instance, usually denote mere quantitative bursts of 'intense polemical activity'[134] in times of political strife. Conversely, pamphletary 'clusters' are scholarly abstractions: they extract raw polemical matter from contingent historical situations to produce the kinds of thematic groupings that make up literary anthologies and handbooks.[135]

Pamphletary 'waves' are both more familiar and more interesting – historically, conceptually, and metaphorically. They are also coupled to other chronological subdivisions, most prominent among which are the successive 'waves' of the feminist movement, despite several noted critiques of this metaphor.[136] Yet the fact that the US-American feminist movement's

---

[133] C. Junker, 'Claiming Class: The Manifesto between Categorical Disruption and Stabilisation', *Culture, Theory and Critique*, vol. 63, no. (2–3), pp. 189–205. See also: C. Arruzza, T. Bhattacharya, N. Fraser, *Feminism for the 99%: A Manifesto*, (Verso, 2019), pp. 5–14.

[134] My translation. F. Lordon, 'La paille et la poutre', *Le Monde diplomatique*, 24.08.2012, https://blog.mondediplo.net/2012-08-24-Conspirationnisme-la-paille-et-la-poutre.

[135] A. Hasenbank, 'Formal Protest: Reconsidering the Poetics of Canadian Pamphleteering', B. Vautour, E. Wunker, T. V. Mason, C. Verduyn, eds., *Public Poetics: Critical Issues in Canadian Poetry and Poetics*, (Wilfrid Laurier University Press, 2015), pp. 231–252. See also: K. Yang, *Analysing Intersectionality: A Toolbox of Methods*, (Sage, 2023).

[136] B. Thompson, 'Multiracial Feminism: Recasting the Chronology of Second Wave Feminism', *Feminist Studies*, Summer, 2002, vol. 28, no. 2, pp. 336–360.

own 'mythological'[137] origins are often traced back to the Seneca Falls Convention and its pamphletary *Declaration of Sentiments* (1848) remains significant for both literary and political history.[138] The 'waves' of the Women's Movement, whatever the appropriateness of the metaphor for the reconstruction of feminist history through print cultures[139], have all been accompanied by cyclical waves of pamphletary texts: 'waves' therefore denote the coupling of polemical writing and social history. What is the modality of this coupling, and how can we theorize the way publics and texts coalesce into historical 'movements' or 'pressure groups'[140]?

First, waves are cyclical in the precise Darntonian sense that is usually brushed over in Book History. Pamphletary waves not only address a text to a public, but also a public to a text and its author. What Darnton loosely describes as the 'general sense of the literary enterprise'[141] is perhaps most clearly perceptible when publics exert their political agency through the very act of identifying, selecting, sharing, commenting, and often rewriting pamphletary texts among a host of possible texts, thus

V. Hersford, *Feeling Women's Liberation*, (Duke University Press, 2013), pp. 1–24. M. V. Rowley, 'The Idea of Ancestry: Of Feminist Genealogies and Many Other Things', C. McCann, S. Kim, eds., *Feminist Theory Reader: Local and Global Perspectives*, (Routledge, 2016), pp. 77–83.

[137] L. Tetrault, *The Myth of Seneca Falls: Memory and the Women's Suffrage Movement, 1848–1898*, (The University of North Carolina Press, 2014), p. 2.

[138] J. Wellman, *The Road to Seneca Falls: Elizabeth Cady Stanton and the First Woman's Rights Convention*, (University of Illinois Press, 2004). D. Bebnowski, 'Pressing Social Orders', in P.-H. Monot, D. Bebnowski, S. Gröppmaier, eds., *Activist Writing: History, Politics, Rhetoric*, (Intercom, 2024), pp. 115–127. D. Bebnowski, 'Radikaler Druck – Druckerzeugnisse und Radikalitäten in der zweiten Welle des Feminismus in den USA', *Österreichische Zeitschrift für Geschichtswissenschaften*, vol. 35, no. 1 (2024), pp. 70–95.

[139] A. Beins, *Liberation in Print: Feminist Periodicals and Social Movement Identity*, (University of Georgia Press, 2017), pp. 1–15.

[140] M. Olson, *The Logic of Collective Action*, (Harvard University Press, 2002), pp. 132–133.

[141] R. Darnton, 'What is the History of Books?', *Daedalus*, vol. 111, no. 3, pp. 65–83, 67.

Pamphleteering 51

funnelling political and literary agency from authors and publishers to reading publics – and back.

Second, waves are cyclical in a loosely historical sense. The feminist movement is a particularly telling example of the way pamphletary texts relate intertextually to pamphlets published during earlier waves of the movement. The classic polemical texts of the successive feminist waves all refer, with varying degrees of explicitness, to previous phases, texts, and positions, thereby maintaining a collective archive of dissent, affects,[142] and polemical strategies to be, in effect, *recycled* by future social actors.

To take an almost classic example, Valerie Solanas's relentless attacks on the intersection of '*Money, Marriage and Prostitution*'[143] in the *SCUM Manifesto* (1967) rephrased and radicalized the Suffragette's criticism of marriage of the early twentieth century.[144] Solanas's polemic would in turn make several reappearances in the defining texts of the Queer Movement published during the HIV/AIDS epidemic. Notably, the pamphlet *Queers Read This*, distributed in the 'tens of thousands'[145] by the activist group Queer Nation during the June 1990 Gay Pride Parades in New York City and Chicago, adapted the first- and second-wave feminist critique of marriage for nascent queer counterpublics. It also drew on the *SCUM Manifesto*'s incendiary tone to propose core strategic measures:

> I want there to be a moratorium on straight marriage, on babies, on public displays of affection among the opposite sex and media images that promote heterosexuality. Until

---

[142] Generally: K. T. Flannery, *Feminist Literacies, 1968–1975*, (University of Illinois Press, 2005), pp. 65–69.

[143] V. Solanas, S.C.U.M. (Society for Cutting up Men) Manifesto, (Olympia Press, 1967), p. 8.

[144] Generally: C. Simmons, *Making Marriage Modern: Women's Sexuality from the Progressive Era to World War II*, (Oxford University Press, 2009); R. E. Lennon, *Wedded Wife: A Feminist History of Marriage*, (Quarto, 2023); M. L. Shanley, *Feminism, Marriage, and the Law in Victorian England*, (Princeton University Press, 1989).

[145] J. Tierney, 'Throngs Cheer at Gay and Lesbian March', *New York Times*, 25 June 1990, section B, page 1.

> I can enjoy the same freedom of movement and sexuality, as straights, their privilege must stop and it must be given over to me and my queer sisters and brothers.
>
> Straight people will not do this voluntarily and so they must be forced into it. Straights must be frightened into it. Terrorized into it. Fear is the most powerful motivator. No one will give us what we deserve. Rights are not given they are taken, by force if necessary.[146]

Queer Nation's rhetoric at once entered mainstream media outlets and feminist historiography, most notably through Rebecca Walker's short pamphlet 'Becoming the 3rd Wave', published in the high-circulation magazine *Ms.* in 1992. Here, Walker drew conclusions from Anita Hill's accusations of sexual harassment against Supreme Court Justice Clarence Thomas. As a response to the outcome of the widely publicized confirmation hearings, Walker reiterated the oppositional logic and rhetorical violence of second-wave critiques of matrimony:

> Let Thomas's confirmation serve to remind you, as it did me, that the fight is far from over. Let the dismissal of a woman's experience move you to anger. Turn that outrage into political power. Do not vote for them unless they work for us. Do not have sex with them, do not break bread with them, do not nurture them if they don't prioritize our freedom to control our bodies and our lives.
>
> I am not a postfeminist feminist. I am the Third Wave.[147]

---

[146] P.-H. Monot, ed., 'Queers Read This: The Queer Nation Manifesto: A Commented Edition with Contextual Sources and a Facsimile Copy of the Original Pamphlet' (Version 1.0), in P.-H. Monot, ed., *The Arts of Autonomy: A Living Anthology of Polemical Literature*, (The Arts of Autonomy, 2024), p. 14. https://artsautonomy.hypotheses.org.

[147] R. Walker, 'Becoming the 3rd Wave', *Ms.* (Magazine), Spring 2002; 12/2, pp. 86–87, 87.

A particular sense of historicity emerges from the polemical writings of the feminist movement. These texts not only constitute one of the main historical archives of US-American and transnational feminism, both quantitatively and politically, they also give prominence to its strategic cohesiveness, or strategic 'permanency'.[148] Feminist pamphleteering is an 'idiom of resistance',[149] that is, a group of propositions established and recognized through usage as having a political meaning and value. By referring successive 'waves' to one another, feminist polemics draw attention not only to progress made,[150] but also to the permanence of injustice and, in turn, to a strategic need for pamphleteering: 'the fight is far from over' and can only be waged in the margins of public discourse.[151] This logic has been accompanied by the development of a dedicated print infrastructure: 'feminists needed not merely a room, but an entire print culture of their own if they hoped to communicate among themselves and spread their ideas to a larger public.'[152]

Finally, 'waves' are cyclical in that they are subject to complex dynamic phases. Polemical texts and their adjacent movements are born, ascend, and finally collapse, following rising and diving flows of political animus.[153] Between trough and crest, political aspirations are consolidated through accumulation, comparison, and mutual reinforcement (here, the colloquial lexicon of associative dissent is highly varied, ranging from mere mutual

---

[148] H. J. McCammon, M. Moon, 'Social Movement Coalitions', in D. Della Porta, M. Diani, eds., *The Oxford Handbook of Social Movements*, (Oxford University Press, 2015), pp. 326–339, p. 327.

[149] K. C. Pearce, 'The Radical Feminist Manifesto as Generic Appropriation: Gender, Genre, And Second Wave Resistance', *Southern Journal of Communication*, vol. 64, no.4 (1999), pp. 307–315.

[150] K. K. Janus, 'Finding Common Feminist Ground: The Role of the Next Generation in Shaping Feminist Legal Theory', *Duke Journal of Gender Law & Policy*, Vol. 20, no.255 (2013), pp. 255–285.

[151] R. Walker, 'Becoming the 3rd Wave', *Ms.* (Magazine), Spring 2002; vol. 12, no. 2, pp. 86–87, 87.

[152] T. Travis, 'The Women in Print Movement: History and Implications', *Book History*, vol. 11 (2008), pp. 275–300, p. 282.

[153] S. Helmreich, *A Book of Waves*, (Duke University Press, 2023), pp. 4–30.

'support' and 'hope' to 'consciousness raising' and '*mass* consciousness-raising', with respective pamphlets for each entry[154]). As metaphors for the mutability of political agency, waves have therefore entered the imaginary of profane political theory, from Gustave Courbet's obsessive depiction of waves during the Paris Commune (1871) and its popular fervour to the fabled 'democratic waves'[155] that have surged in the wake of the Revolutions of 1989. Since the 1850s, however, the feminist movement has insisted on a precious amendment to this tradition: waves necessarily depend on written dissent to become politically effective.

5.2 The GI Underground Press

To become politically effective, pamphlets and pamphletary waves also need to reach a constituency and a public. How do texts address, create, or maintain publics on whose behalf they call out injustices and argue for normative changes? More to the point, how do highly heterogeneous, sometimes segregated[156] and antagonized reading publics agree to coalesce around common pamphletary demands?

In this section, I focus on the GI Underground Press to explore the 'constituent power'[157] of pamphlets in the face of highly diverse readerships and, just as frequently, highly diverse authorships. These polemical newsletters, short newspapers, and single-page pamphlets were mainly written by active-duty GIs, recently discharged troops, and deserters. They circulated widely yet did so without the approval of military authorities. While

---

[154] See for instance: K. Sarachild, 'A Program for Feminist "Consciouness Raising"', in S. Firestone, A. Koedt, eds., *Notes from the Second Year: Women's Liberation. Major Writings of the Radical Feminists*, (Radical Feminism, 1970), pp. 78–80.

[155] C. Mouffe, *The Return of the Political*, (Verso, 1993), p. 23.

[156] I use the term in its historical sense to refer to the de jure segregation of African Americans from whites based on racial categorizations until the Voting Rights Act of 1965.

[157] R. Houghton, A. O'Donoghue, 'Manifestos as Constituent Power: Performing a Feminist Revolution', *Global Constitutionalism*, vol. 12, no. 3 (2023), pp. 412–437.

the *News Notes* of the Central Committee for Conscientious Objectors were first issued in 1949, the vast majority of the GI Underground periodicals and single-issue publications were created during the nineteen-year Vietnam War (November 1955–April 1975). With the increased presence of U.S. troops coming ashore in Vietnam from 1965 onwards, the regional demographics of combatant and support troops changed radically, with African Americans, whites, Asian Americans, Pacific Islanders, Native Americans, Hispanic American men and women now fighting under a common leadership.[158] The GI Underground Press reflected and politicized this juxtaposition, which was unprecedented in U.S. American military history: the Vietnam War was the first American war in which African American and white troops were not segregated.

Scholarship knows comparatively little of the circa 900 underground periodicals published during the Vietnam War era. Their status as 'periodicals', or even as 'printed material', was doubtful: most were mimeographed copies of hand-lettered manuscripts and drawings. This ambiguity was also a matter of immediate legal import: Department of Defense (DoD) Directive 1325.6 (*Guidelines for Handling Dissident and Protest Activities among Members of the Armed Forces*) stipulated that while 'the mere possession of unauthorized printed material may not be prohibited, printed material that is prohibited from distribution shall be impounded',[159] a sentence most GI Underground publications would include in their masthead.

GI Underground publications shared crucial features with revolutionary pamphleteering. All but a few of their contributors wrote anonymously. Their circulation was difficult to gauge, their material footprint was erratic, ranging from barely readable single-sheet prints, four-page leaflets, and multiple-section periodicals, their publication frequency varied from

---

[158] D. S. Lucks, *Selma to Saigon: The Civil Rights Movement and the Vietnam War*, (University Press of Kentucky, 2014).

[159] Executive Services Directorate, 'Department of Defense Directive 1325.6', Washington, 7 September 1969. See also: M. Cohn, K. Gilberd, *Rules of Disengagement: The Politics and Honor of Military Dissent*, (New York University Press, 2009), pp. 76–82.

a single issue to more than 800,[160] and their print run varied significantly, ranging from a few hundred to more than 35,000 copies.[161] These publications often used mimeography and hand-lettering as their sole means of production and reproduction. They were the object of constant surveillance by military authorities and intelligence services, which organized frequent search raids, entrapped authors, and enforced 'existing obscenity, drug, and unlicensed vending laws' to circumvent DoD Directive 1325.6 and court-martial contributors, distributors, and readers.[162]

Their general stance was consistently anti-war, anti-militaristic, anti-racist, revolutionary, and anti-imperialist. The aggressiveness of their tone and their ad hominem rhetoric were unmatched in previous GI publications, with one contributor notably describing Secretary of Defense Melvin Laird as a 'a practicing prostitute and pig for the military industrial complex' who was 'proud of his war monger haircut'.[163] Many publications also directly contradicted the strategic imperatives of the Vietnam War by not only encouraging desertion, but also by providing the textual means to do so effectively and safely. Famously, the cover of the June 1971 edition of *Up Against the Bulkhead* provided a bilingual declaration of capitulation to be carried into combat: 'I am against the war and will not fight the Vietnamese people.' The front matter read: 'Clip This to Save Your Life'.[164]

The GI Underground Press would play a decisive, if wholly underestimated, role in the Civil Rights movement by establishing a global

---

[160] R. N. Williams, *The New Exiles: American War Resisters in Canada*, (Liveright, 1971), p. 165.

[161] Department of Defense, Department of Defense Appropriations for 1972, *Hearings before a Subcommittee of the Committee on Appropriations*, Part 4: *Operation and Maintenance*, (U.S. Government Printing Office, 1971), p. 819.

[162] C. Painter, P. Ferrucci, '"Ask What You Can Do to the Army": A Textual Analysis of the Underground GI Press during the Vietnam War", *Media, War & Conflict*, Vol. 12, no. 3 (September 2019), pp. 354–367, p. 364.

[163] See generally: J. Lewes, *Protest and Survive: Underground GI Newspapers during the Vietnam War*, (Praeger, 2003), p. 82.

[164] Anonymous, 'Clip This to Save Your Life', in *Up against the Bulkhead*, vol. 2, no. 3, Issue 8 (June 1971), p. 1. https://content.wisconsinhistory.org/digital/collection/p15932coll8/id/89802.

network of printed political dissent. Underground publications emerged in virtually every location in which the U.S. Army was either stationed or engaged in combat: in Vietnam, in the Philippines, in Australia, in army bases throughout the United States, Germany, France, and Japan, in military prisons, in mess halls, in mailrooms, in immediate combat zones (*The Boomerang Barb* and *GI Says*) and aboard U.S. Navy ships. A contemporary account (1972) directly implicates military authorities and emphasizes the infrastructural precariousness of production aboard ships:

> They try to keep everything from us – they never let us know how many missions the ship flies, how many villages have been wiped out. So we started putting out a paper called *We Are Everywhere*, with statistics about how much ordnance we carry, how many people have been killed. We print it right on the ship and spread it all around. We've had three issues so far, and they can't figure out who's doing it.[165]

Beyond their interest as marginal media, the pamphlets of the GI Underground Press are also a neglected archive that allows us to tell another, complementary story about the Civil Rights Movement. Because they circulated widely and across social boundaries, these texts actively included social actors that were usually excluded from progressive politics. The two known issues of *Women's Voices*, for instance, insisted on the ambiguity of their self-description as a 'pamphlet',[166] simultaneously understood as polemical literature and medical print format (the 'medical pamphlets' of waiting rooms). Published in Okinawa by a group of servicewomen

---

[165] E. Elinson, 'Sailors are Just Cogs in the Bombing Machine: Two Coral Sea Sailors Ashore', *Liberation News Service*, vol. 416, March 4, 1972, p. 1. https://content.wisconsinhistory.org/digital/collection/p15932coll8/id/72983.

[166] Anonymous, 'Alternatives', in *Women's Voices*, vol. 1, no. 1 (1974), pp. 17, p. 17. https://content.wisconsinhistory.org/digital/collection/p15932coll8/id/36388/rec/2.

and civilians, *Women's Voices* not only provided detailed instructions on contraceptives and pregnancy, but also denounced professional and military medicine ('We are dehumanized, chemicalized, analysed and brushed aside'[167]) and encouraged vaginal self-examination as a safe alternative. *Women's Voices* was therefore a medical pamphlet in that it provided condensed practical knowledge, yet it was also a political one in that it turned this knowledge against authorities, wrestled with the injustice imposed upon servicewomen, identified enemies, and encouraged civilians and troops to consider their common interests.

Even more importantly, it advertised (and often imitated in style and content) the seminal 1970/1971 feminist anthology *Our Bodies, Ourselves*: 'We have copies of it at the Women's House and if you can't afford to pay the whole thing we will accept donations'.[168] Such reproductions and recirculations of polemical texts were fixture in the GI Underground Press and enabled texts published in the United States to circulate among highly marginalized publics, most notably African American GIs stationed abroad or deployed in combat zones and as such far removed from the urban settings of 1960s radicalism.

Both *Black Unity*, published at Camp Pendelton (San Diego County), and *A'bout Face 1*, published in Heidelberg and Mannheim (Germany), reprinted Point 6 of the Black Panther Party's pamphletary *Ten-Point Program* (1966): 'We Want All Black Men To Be Exempt From Military Service'.[169] The radical *Voice of the Lumpen*, published in U.S. bases around Frankfurt am Main (Germany), went much further. In the thirteen issues produced between 1971 and 1972, the publication developed a maximalist

---

[167] Anonymous, 'Self Help', in *Women's Voices*, vol. 1, no. 1 (1974), pp. 11–12, p. 11. https://content.wisconsinhistory.org/digital/collection/p15932coll8/id/36382/rec/2.

[168] Anonymous, 'Our Bodies, Ourselves', in *Women's Voices*, vol. 1, no. 1 (1974), p. 4.

[169] G. Jones-Katz, ed., 'Huey P. Newton and Bobby Seale: What We Want Now!, What We Believe: The Black Panther Party Ten-Point Platform and Program', in P.-H. Monot, ed., *The Arts of Autonomy: A Living Anthology of Polemical Literature*, (The Arts of Autonomy, 2022), p. 12.

programme of radical justice and emancipation, pledging to 'move against the evil and corrupt gentry by any means necessary and sufficient',[170] in this way redeploying the rhetoric of Malcolm X's famed 1964 speech at the Organization of Afro-American Unity. By its eighth issue, *Voice of the Lumpen* was reprinting the pamphlets of the Revolutionary People's Communications Network, founded in 1971 in Algeria by Kathleen and Eldridge Cleaver. It highlighted the importance of communication infrastructures and the transnational ambitions of revolutionary anti-militarism, Black anti-fascism, and anti-capitalism:

> The Revolutionary Peoples Communications Network is designed to provide a structure to link up revolutionary organizations and movements operating both inside and outside the United States to circulate and exchange information about the anti-imperialist liberation struggles in which they are engaged. By establishing more coordinated and regular means of communication among ourselves we enhance the ability to coordinate our activities and lay a foundation for a united front.[171]

Political pamphleteering, then, served various functions for dissident troops. It consolidated local movements and provided polemical material for regional, national, or international circulation. It also related the normative claims of militant organizations (such as Point 6 of the *Ten-Point Program*) to the concrete lived experience of African American troops deployed in war zones and, conversely, related their lived experience of combat to abstract normative demands formulated at home. Theory and practice – to use the recurrent terminology of *Voice of the Lumpen* – therefore constituted a system of mutual authentication and legitimation.

---

[170] Anonymous, 'Voice of the Lumpen Manifesto', *Voice of the Lumpen*, vol. 1 (1971), p. 1. www.jstor.org/stable/community.28046308.

[171] International Section of the Black Panther Party, Revolutionary Peoples Communications Network, 'what Is the Revolutionary Peoples Communications Network', *Voice of the Lumpen*, vol. 1, no. 8 (October 1971), p. 2.

Most importantly, GI pamphleteering not only provided marginalized social actors with information and political perspectives, it also allowed them to participate as authors in the elaboration of political strategies. The inaugural issue of the transparently named *FTA* (*Fun Travel Adventure*, Fort Knox), for instance, declared radical openness to be its prime objective: 'We're going to say what most of us say when talking to each other but we're going to put it in print.'[172] Others, like *Highway 13*, consisted primarily of readers' letters that denounced both 'racism' and the 'censorship' of critical statements by GIs about the 'military-industrial complex'.[173] *Voice of the Lumpen*, without doubt one of the most uncompromising and polarizing publications of the Civil Rights era, also repeatedly called for readers to send in material:

> In our struggle for freedom, we must combat many evil forces. One of these forces is a very powerful news media which is used by the fascist ruling class against the people, against the people's just struggle. So it was necessary to create an alternate media, a people's media. The Voice of the Lumpen newspaper is the voice of the people and the G.I. community.
>
> The people must have a means to express their true wants, needs, and desires. In order for the Voice of the Lumpen to function, the people must support it, not only by reading it but by contributing community news. We ask the people of the GI community, to bring or mailin news articles to the Voice of the Lumpen, 6 Frankfurt/Main, Adalbertstr. 6.[174]

---

[172] Anonymous, 'Editorial Policy', *Fun Travel Adventure*, vol. 1 (23 June 1968), pp. 1–2, p. 1. https://content.wisconsinhistory.org/digital/collection/p15932coll8/id/42075.

[173] Anonymous, 'GIs & Workers Fight Racism', *Highway 13*, vol. 1, no. 6 (July–August 1873), pp. 1–10, p. 1. www.jstor.org/stable/pdf/community.28038376.pdf.

[174] Anonymous, 'Editor's Statement', *Voice of the Lumpen*, vol. 1/4 (1971), p. 8. www.jstor.org/stable/community.28046313.

The construction of an authorial collectivity, of 'the people', of a 'most of us' (*FTA*), or of what Mary Ann Caws calls the '*we*-speak'[175] inherent to all polemical writing, is therefore dependent on the active participation of the readership and, conversely, the exclusion of the 'the brass', the 'fascists' and 'pigs' that make up 'Amerikkka'.[176] Therein lies the 'constituent power'[177] of GI pamphleteering: it provided rational grounds on which the objective heterogeneity of its readership and collective authorship could be downplayed. In fact, the GI Underground press expressly insisted on the universality of its political stances when – and especially when – its content was addressed to specific political factions or subgroups: *Voice of the Lumpen* emphasized its compatibility with feminist critique, the Resisters Inside the Army's two-page periodical *ACT* advocated for solidarity between 'Black' GIs and 'Yellow' Vietnamese fighters against a government that was 'racist – inside and outside the States',[178] *Bragg Briefs* (Fayetteville, NC) built a platform that was inclusive of veterans, deserters, the Women' Army Corps, GIs 'using hard drugs',[179] lesbians, 'gay and straight alike'.[180]

Beyond the immediate political affordances of 'universalist' positions (notably the maximization of readership, as well as the numerical growth and consolidation of politicized social actors), the radical inclusiveness of even the most explicitly partisan GI publications can perhaps best be explained by the military culture's own nominally 'universalist' material underpinnings: universal conscription. In fact, the justification of the

---

[175] M. A. Caws, 'The Poetics of the Manifesto: Nowness and Newness', in M. A. Caws, ed., *Manifesto: A Century of Isms*, (University of Nebraska Press, 2001), pp. xix–xxxi, p. xx.

[176] This terminology is so abundant in the GI Underground Press that I dispense with a specific citation.

[177] R. Houghton, A. O'Donoghue, 'Manifestos as Constituent Power: Performing a Feminist Revolution', *Global Constitutionalism*, vol. 12, no. 3 (2023), pp. 412–437.

[178] Private Cornell Rifleman, 'A better way', *ACT*, vol. 1, no. 1 (1967), p. 1. https://content.wisconsinhistory.org/digital/collection/p15932coll8/id/9797/rec/1.

[179] Anonymous, 'Operation Awareness is Dying', *Bragg Briefs*, vol. 4, no. 5 (June 1971), p. 1. www.jstor.org/stable/community.28034435.

[180] Anonymous, 'Army Uses Scare Tactics against WACs', *Bragg Briefs*, vol. 4, no. 4 (May 1971), p. 6. www.jstor.org/stable/community.28034433.

'practice of coercive mobilization through the notion of universality, the theory that each and every citizen should shoulder an equal share of the nation's military obligation'[181] had become particularly contentious during the Vietnam War. Imbalanced conscription based on racial identity and class, along with 'medical exemptions that favoured the wealthy, student deferments, and the safe haven of the National Guard and Reserves for the upper class'[182] had become central issues in the public perception of the Vietnam War. Criticism of these specific inequalities was a staple in the polemical texts of the GI Underground, thereby both galvanizing dissent *and* encouraging the formation of a more objectively universal, inclusive, and solidary critical constituency. Because they offered a common resistance narrative to a highly heterogeneous readership, and because this common resistance narrative effectively contested the U.S. military's own highly selective uses of universality, the polemical writing of the GI Underground press should not be considered as mere 'media curiosities',[183] but as one of the decisive crucibles of the New Left.[184]

5.3 A Paper Trail to Washington

The Vietnam War habituated several distinct demographics to radical polemic. Countless discharged troops and deserters returned to the United States with expertise in collective pamphleteering, the manufacturing of dissident publications, and the covert circulation of prohibited texts. Of those innumerable civilians who had either read or written for the GI

---

[181] S. W. Currin Jr., *An Army of the Willing: Fayette'Nam, Soldier Dissent, and the Untold Story of the All-Volunteer Force*, (Dissertation, Duke University, 2015), p. 23. https://dukespace.lib.duke.edu/server/api/core/bitstreams/8cbcdadb-75f5-4588-9bfa-184adb926743/content.

[182] *Ibid.*, p. 25.

[183] D. Seidman, 'Paper Soldiers: The *Ally* and the GI Underground Press during the Vietnam War', J. L. Baughman, J. Ratner-Rosenhagen, J. P. Dansky, eds., *Protest on the Page: Essays on Print and the Culture of Dissent Since 1865*, (The University of Wisconsin Press, 2015), pp. 183–202, p. 185.

[184] See also: S. Kouvelakis, *Philosophy and Revolution: From Kant to Marx*, (Verso, 2018), pp. 256–267.

Underground Press, many returned to careers in academia, management, and administration, both in the United States and in Europe.[185] Yet these troops and civilians were not only 'media pioneers'[186] in that they deployed an intercontinental network of pamphleteers, lay publishers, and partisan readers. They also pioneered a way of actively participating in democratic processes by way of marginal media infrastructures.

In effect, the publications of the GI Underground bore witness to a drastic transformation of the way marginalized social actors assessed their own capacity to question legal norms, exert political power, and call into question what sociologist Luc Boltanski calls the 'reality of reality'.[187] Why, in effect, 'did these soldiers presume that they had rights protected by the First Amendment when their predecessors had resented but essentially accepted the Uniform Code of Military Justice?'[188] Signs that collective exercises in radical pamphleteering were instrumental in this shift had first become apparent far removed from the battlefield. Underground and clandestine publications were springing up in the San Francisco Bay Area as in much of the United States. Long before the *Queer Nation Manifesto*'s insistence on four-letter words (the classic triumvirate of 'fuck', 'cunt', and 'dick', along with a litany of 'ass'[189]), the *Berkeley Barb* (1965–1980), *The Great Speckled Bird* (1968–1976, 1988–1990), the *San Francisco Oracle* (1966–1968), and the *Chicago Seed* (1967–1974) mixed unrestrained rhetoric with anti-war politics, psychedelic advocacy, erotic art, radical agitation, and the polemical writings of discharged troops. By the late 1960s,

---

[185] M. Höhn, 'The Black Panther Solidarity Committees and the Voice of the Lumpen', *German Studies Review*, vol. 31, no. 1 (February 2008), pp. 133–154.

[186] K. Wachsberger, 'Foreword', in K. Wachsberger, ed., *Insider Histories of the Vietnam Era Underground Press*, vol. 1, (Michigan State University Press, 2011), pp. xiii–xv, p. xiv.

[187] L. Boltanski, *On Critique: A Sociology of Emancipation*, (Polity Press, 2011), p. 107.

[188] B. Tischler, 'Breaking Ranks: GI Antiwar Newspapers and the Culture of Protest', *Vietnam Generation*, vol. 2, no. 1, Article 4, pp. 20–50, 21.

[189] P.-H. Monot, ed., 'Queers Read This: The Queer Nation Manifesto: A Commented Edition with Contextual Sources and a Facsimile Copy of the Original Pamphlet' (Version 1.0), in P.-H. Monot, ed., *The Arts of Autonomy: A Living Anthology of Polemical Literature*, (The Arts of Autonomy, 2024), p. 9. https://artsautonomy.hypotheses.org.

a transnational network of radical, short-form, polemical publications was established, posing new challenges to state institutions and political opponents alike.

It is no exaggeration to say that polemical literature, both at home and on the battlefield, was one of the key reasons for the modernization and expansion of the state surveillance of political radicals. While previous administrations from the First Red Scare (1919) onwards had controlled dissent on an ad hoc basis, orchestrating harassment campaigns against targeted groups and individuals, the Lyndon B. Johnson and Richard Nixon administrations successively coordinated efforts to create a unified surveillance infrastructure. By the 1950s, the FBI under Hoover had compiled a 'Security Index' listing up to 15,000 individuals (ranging from polemicists and communists to clergymen and public figures such as Martin Luther King, Jr.) to be immediately arrested in case of a national emergency. For the first time, this 'custodial detention list'[190] was stored on IBM cards, ushering in the era of digital mass surveillance. By 1967, the programme was supplemented by a 'Rabble Rouser Index' (later renamed 'Agitator Index'), a computerized database of 200,000 activists and writers[191] 'who have demonstrated by their actions and speeches that they have a propensity for fomenting racial disorder',[192] a definition soon to be expanded to include any 'person who tries to arouse people to violent action by appealing to their emotions, prejudices, etc.; a demagogue'.[193] Through electronic surveillance, campus infiltrations, break-ins, and systematic harassment, state

---

[190] S. Rosenfeld, *Subversives: The FBI's War on Student Radicals, and Reagan's Rise to Power*, (Farrar, Straus, and Giroux, 2012), pp. 69–76.

[191] M. Linfield, *Freedom under Fire: U.S. Civil Liberties in Times of War*, (South End Press, 1990), pp. 136–140.

[192] L. B. Johnson, SAC Letter 67–47, 4 April 1967, https://ia601007.us.archive.org/14/items/FBIRabbleRouserAgitatorIndexHQ1577782Sections14/FBI%20Rabble%20Rouser-Agitator%20Index%20-%20HQ%20157–7782%2C%20sections%201–4.pdf.

[193] L. B. Johnson, SAC Letter 67–70, 28 November 1967, https://ia601007.us.archive.org/14/items/FBIRabbleRouserAgitatorIndexHQ1577782Sections14/FBI%20Rabble%20Rouser-Agitator%20Index%20-%20HQ%20157–7782%2C%20sections%201–4.pdf.

authorities tightened their grip around what they had come to perceive as a major threat to domestic peace, orderly political discourse, capital interests, and racial segregation.[194]

Now treated as a grave danger necessitating staunch coercive measures, pamphletary publics were in turn given legitimate reasons to take themselves seriously as a political force. In other words, it is the expansion of surveillance itself that made it possible for pamphletary publics to perceive themselves as part of an agential group endowed with real political power.[195] Importantly, the increased surveillance measures also taught writers and activists to think of themselves as collective agents: they were precisely as general, universal, or undifferentiated as surveillance measures implied and codified legally. It is therefore not surprising that the pamphlets of the Civil War era repeatedly formulated demands in the name of collective subjects, long before the minute segmentation of activist groups was to take hold in the following decades: 'we', 'kids', 'this generation', 'women', 'human beings', as well as various shared pseudonyms or 'assemblages of enunciation'[196] were the collective subjects who demanded rights by pamphletary means. Thus, we can best think of pamphleteering during the Civil Rights Era as a wide-ranging set of social and moral dispositions that included not only a generous universalizing tendency among writers and readers, but also state infrastructures that made this tendency appear to be inevitable and justified in the eyes of these writers and readers themselves. The 'subjectification through reading' and 'subjectification through writing',[197] an arduous process of self-definition and self-clarification that occurs whenever social actors turn to texts to define and defend their

---

[194] G. Rips, 'The Campaign against the Underground Press', in A. Janowitz, N. A. Peters, eds., *Unamerican Activities: Pen American Center Report*, (City Lights Bookstore, 1981), pp. 37–158, p. 56.

[195] See also: M. Puchner, *Poetry of the Revolution: Marx, Manifestos, and the Avant-Gardes*, (Princeton University Press, 2006), pp. 3–7.

[196] M. Deseriis, 'On the Symbolic Power of Shared Pseudonyms', *Seachange*, vol. 6, no. 1 (2015), pp. 51–62, p. 59.

[197] My paraphrase. A. Reckwitz, *Das hybride Subjekt: Eine Theorie der Subjektkulturen von der bürgerlichen Moderne zur Postmoderne*, (Suhrkamp, 2020), p. 169, 177.

political existence, thereby brings into relief an important universalizing logic of collective action that is often overlooked in histories of the Civil Rights Movement and the New Left. This amendment to the (overall justified) insistence on identity politics and anti-universalism in the seminal accounts[198] of the late 1960s is what Book History in general, and the study of polemical literature in particular, can contribute to the history of the Civil Rights Movement.

Yet while the state and its coercive measures did have a formative effect on the pamphletary cultures of the Civil Rights Era, the reverse is also true, albeit in more isolated terms. A fascinating example of a pamphlet having a crucial effect on policy, nationally and internationally, emerged from a protracted process of collective writing and rewriting. In 1972, the Trail of Broken Treaties cross-country caravan took Indigenous organizations from Seattle, San Francisco, and Los Angeles to Washington, D.C., where they presented a seminal *20-Point Position Paper* to President Richard Nixon. Quite literally, 'textuality [was] dragged into the streets'[199] by the cross-country caravan of the American Indian Movement (AIM). Along the way, thousands of Native Americans put their demands to paper, revising the collective draft during workshops that aimed at defining 'one basic status for all Indians, which could be easily understood by all Indians and which could not be whittled away by the actions of the different states'.[200]

The central objective of the *20-Point Position Paper* was to restore and secure treaty-making authority by Indian Tribes. The text demonstrated AIM's readiness to deal with federal institutions on almost formalistic terms, often showcasing an intimate technical understanding of the institutional underpinnings of Native American history. Discussions of expropriation, displacement, and cultural marginalization were phrased in legal terms, rather than ethical ones. In conjunction with the seventy-one-day siege of

---

[198] A. Hartman, *A War for the Soul of America: A History of the Culture Wars*, (Chicago University Press, 2019).

[199] T. L. Ebert, 'Manifesto as Theory and Theory as Material Force: Toward a Red Polemic', *JAC*, vol. 23, no. 3 (2003), pp. 553–562, p. 553.

[200] V. Deloria, Jr., *Behind the Trail of Broken Treaties: An Indian Declaration of Independence*, (University of Texas Press, 1984), p. 50.

Wounded Knee, South Dakota, in 1973, during which two activists were killed, the American Indian Movement's pamphlet durably radicalized the strategies of the Indigenous movement.[201] Yet the highly ambiguous nature of the pamphlet reflected the Civil Rights Movement's own contradictions regarding the place of universality. On the one hand, AIM proclaimed the generality, inclusivity, and rationality of its core demands:

> We seek a new American majority – a majority that is not content merely to confirm itself by superiority in numbers, but which by conscience is committed toward prevailing upon the public will in ceasing wrongs and in doing right. For our part, in words and deeds of coming days, we propose to produce a rational, reasoned manifesto for construction of an Indian future in America. If America has maintained faith with its original spirit, or may recognize it now, we should not be denied.[202]

On the other hand, however, AIM's insistence on autonomy and treaty-making authority *excluded* the kind of universalist leanings that had become apparent in the Underground press of the mid-1960s: 'Unlike the American civil rights movement, with which it has been compared, AIM has seen self-determination and racism differently. Desegregation was not a goal. Individual rights were not placed ahead of the preservation of Native Nation sovereignty.'[203]

---

[201] J. W. Sayer, *Ghost Dancing the Law: The Wounded Knee Trials*, (Harvard University Press, 1997), p. 16–31; T. R. Johnson, *The Occupation of Alcatraz Island: Indian Self-determination and the Rise of Indian Activism*, (University of Illinois Press, 1996), pp. 223–224.

[202] I have written about the AIM manifesto in the past and am repeating some observations made in: P.-H. Monot, ed. '*The Trail of Broken Treaties 20-Point Position Paper: An Indian Manifesto*. A Commented Edition with Contextual Sources' in (Version 1.0), P.-H. Monot, ed., *The Arts of Autonomy: A Living Anthology of Polemical Literature*, (The Arts of Autonomy, 2022), p. 15.

[203] L. W. Wittstock, E. J. Salinas, 'A Brief History of the American Indian Movement', www.aimovement.org/ggc/history.html. See also: A. M. Josephy

It is arguably this very ambiguity that sealed the fate of the *20-Point Position Paper*, as it unwittingly provided a framework for larger-scale institutional projects that faced similar contradictions. First, AIM's principal demands were voiced once again at the crucial International NGO Conference on Discrimination Against Indigenous People in the Americas, held in the United Nations' offices in Geneva on 20–23 September 1977. It was the first UN conference at which Native peoples could present Indigenous delegates. The Conference's own manifesto, the *Declaration Of Principles for the Defense of the Indigenous Nations and Peoples of the Western Hemisphere*, a core text in the political history of Indigenous Nations, rephrased AIM's fundamental demands, including those concerning the treaty-making sovereignty of Indigenous peoples.[204] Second, the *20-Point Position Paper* served as a basis for the 2007 *United Nations Declaration on the Rights of Indigenous Peoples*, which defined minimal legal provisions. They included basic cultural, educational, economic, and linguistic rights for Indigenous peoples. The importance of the *20-Point Position Paper* has been noted by the UN itself, highlighting its influence on preparatory studies published as early as 1982.[205] Finally, the *20-Point Position Paper* forced the FBI and CIA to implement 'an intensified effort to identify violence-prone individuals or organizations within the American Indian movement' and to deploy an 'informant development program'[206] to infiltrate communities and their political structures. After a seventy-one-day siege and the finalization of the *20-Point Position Paper*, AIM was evicted from

Jr., J. Nagel, T. Johnson, eds., *Red Power: The American Indians' Fight for Freedom*, (University of Nebraska Press, 1999), pp. 22–26.

[204] See also: K. Engle, *The Elusive Promise of Indigenous Development: Rights, Culture, Strategy*, (Duke University Press, 2010), pp. 73–76, as well as: S. J. Anaya, *Indigenous Peoples in International Law*, (Oxford University Press, 2007), pp. 77–79.

[205] For instance, in the 'Study on the Problem of Discrimination Against Indigenous Populations', published by the United Nations Economic and Social Council on 12 July 1982. The full report is available on the United Nations' website. www.un.org/esa/socdev/unpfii/documents/MCS_xix_en.pdf.

[206] FBI Memorandum on the American Indian Movement calling for the implementation of an informant development program, 27 November 1972, Federal Bureau of Investigation Library.

Pamphleteering 69

the Bureau of Indian Affairs it had been occupying. AIM organizer Dennis Banks summarizes the events:

> The government bribed us to leave with promises that were broken almost as soon as they were made. They promised to 'seriously' consider our twenty demands but soon 'officially and formally' rejected all of them. They promised not to prosecute Trail members for actions taken during the occupation, but broke this promise too, claiming their agreement did not cover the 'theft of government property', the documents we had seized. The Trail of Broken Treaties ended as a trail of broken promises.[207]

Despite this failure, the *20-Point Position Paper* was immensely successful. While it is generally the case, as Michael Warner argues, that 'no single text can create a public ... since a public is understood to be an ongoing space of encounter for discourse', and while 'texts themselves do not create publics, but the concatenation of texts through time',[208] most exceptions to this rule are historically significant – from Luther's *Ninety-Five Theses* and Zola's *J'Accuse . . . !* to AIM's *20-Point Position Paper*. As 'effective knowledge', as 'a vigilant form of intervention into existing knowledges',[209] AIM's decisive pamphlet forced the state to take note of the power a single text could deploy among marginalized populations. For a time, the *20-Point Position Paper* reverted the relationship between state authorities and pamphletary publics, demonstrating that pamphlets and pamphleteers were endowed with a crucial function not only in the formation of politicized reading (and writing) publics, but also in the elaboration and contestation of politics in its most institutional form.

---

[207] D. Banks, R. Erdoes, *Ojibwa Warrior: Dennis Banks and the Rise of the American Indian Movement*, (University of Oklahoma Press, 2004), p. 143.

[208] M. Warner, 'Publics and Counterpublics', *Public Culture*, vol. 14/1 (2002), pp. 49–90, p. 62.

[209] T. L. Ebert, 'Manifesto as Theory and Theory as Material Force: Toward a Red Polemic', *JAC*, vol. 23, no. 3 (2003), pp. 553–562, p. 554, 558.

6 Pamphleteering after Paper

6.1 1988 and the Return of 'Virality'

In this section, I want to make the case that Book History and the history of pamphleteering have something to say about the radicalization of public speech online. Social scientists and critics of the contemporary public sphere ought to consider the rise of invective speech, ad hominem attacks, and radical critique in light of their infrastructural and generic origins: pamphleteering. I also want to argue that one of the important tropes in internet culture, 'virality', can best be understood – and criticized – with reference to its origins in pamphletary culture.

In 1988, the institutional framework of the future World Wide Web was established,[210] the first commercial Internet Service Providers were capitalized, daunting technical problems of data flow were solved, and the Morris Worm appeared, the first computer virus spread via the internet rather than floppy disks. It was also the first to garner the attention of the non-specialist press.

By 1991, engineers and investors were drafting the technological and capitalistic contours of 'Web 1.0' and Jeremy Rifkin was contemplating the cultural impact of the coming 'Age of Access'.[211] In turn, public discussions of polemical speech and pamphleteering were embedded into a new technological lexicon. Justice Clarence Thomas (see Section 5.1) compared his confirmation hearings with a 'high-tech lynching',[212] while the concept of 'virality' itself escaped the epistemic confines of epidemiology to now serve

---

[210] Notably during the conference at Harvard's Kennedy School of Government on 'The Commercialization and Privatization of the Internet'. B. Frischmann, 'Privatization and Commercialization of the Internet Infrastructure: Rethinking Market Intervention into Government and Government Intervention into the Market', *Columbia Science and Technology Law Review*, vol. 2 (2001). www.columbia.edu/cu/stlr/html/volume2/frischmann.pdf.

[211] J. Rifkin, *The Age of Access: The New Culture of Hypercapitalism*, (Penguin, 2001).

[212] H. V. Davis, 'The High-tech Lynching and the High-tech Overseer: Thoughts from the Anita Hill/Clarence Thomas Affair', *The Black Scholar*, vol. 22, no. 1/2, (Winter 1991–Spring 1992), pp. 27–29.

Pamphleteering 71

as a general metaphor for the high-frequency circulation of digital data. By the mid-1990s, 'virality' had become internet culture's own profane theory of cultural transmission, as witnessed by the emergence of an informal canon of short-form, digital, high-circulation ('viral') pamphlets on digitalization, virality, and free speech: John Perry Barlow's *A Declaration of the Independence of Cyberspace* (1996), the *Cluetrain Manifesto* (1999), The Pirate Bay's *POwr, Broccoli and Kopimi* (2005), Piotr Czerski's *We, the Web Kids* (2012), the collectively authored *A Feminist Server* (2014), and James Damore's *Google's Ideological Echo Chamber* (2017).[213]

These pamphlets discuss internet politics, net neutrality, filesharing, freeware, and recruiting policies in the tech industry from a wide spectrum of ideological perspectives. Importantly, and for the first time in the history of pamphletary literature, none of these texts existed as print media. In fact, most of them do not even depend on a specific format: they are mere semiotic strings (often in plain .TXT or .RTF formats) that elicit dedicated interpretative dispositions for dedicated digital and social uses. Some are distributed as attachments to pirated video and music files on sharing platforms, thus maximizing circulation and, perhaps, the serendipity of protest: 'virality' consolidates incidental social structures into pamphletary publics.[214]

Yet 'virality', as a conceptual device and as a communicational property, is itself deeply embedded into the history of polemical literature. The term 'virus', in the sense of an infectious pathogen, has been in use since the early eighteenth century, long before the formal discovery of viruses by Dmitiri Ivanovsky in 1892. During the eighteenth and nineteenth centuries, both medical practitioners and polemical authors routinely commented (and punned[215]) on the

---

[213] These pamphlets have been collected in: M. Schmalstieg, B. Crevits, V. Kruug, eds., *Manifestos for the Internet Age*, (sine loco) 2016.

[214] I am summarizing from: P.-H. Monot, 'Poor, Nasty, British, and Short. Contemporary Pamphleteering, Popular Literacy, and the Politics of Literary Circulation', in M. Gamper, J. Müller-Tamm, D. Wachter, J. Wrobel, eds., *Der Wert der literarischen Zirkulation / The Value of Literary Circulation*, (Springer, 2023), pp. 173–185.

[215] Benjamin Franklin: 'I had *caught* [disputatiousness] by reading my father's books of dispute about religion. Persons of good sense, I have since observed,

similarity between the spread of disease and the spread of polemic. The Boston Smallpox Epidemic of 1721, for instance, which infected more than half of a population of 11,000 and which was then known to involve a 'communicable' disease, saw the unfolding of a large-scale pamphlet war between proponents of vaccination and proponents of inoculation. Andrew Gross has shown how this pamphlet war subsequently triggered a series of public debates about the properties and ideological makeup of the early American public sphere, its counterpublics, and the weight they respectively attributed to rational debate. Gross concludes that 'the infection metaphor is not very useful for making sense of the cultural significance of contagion. The transmission patterns of a virus are in no way analogous to the publication infrastructures that transmit meaning'.[216]

Yet during the nineteenth and twentieth centuries, this conflation of viral and pamphletary 'contagion' would not only become increasingly entrenched in public discourse, but it would also repeatedly ignite further pamphlet wars. All the main viral events of the time would be accompanied by a trail of short-form polemical texts, from Oliver Wendell Holmes, Sr.'s diatribes against the obstetricians of New England (the 'Synod of Accoucheurs',[217] as he eloquently puts it) during the height of the puerperal fever epidemic to the countless pamphlets published the Covid-19 pandemic variously incriminating Chinese authorities[218] or reactivating antisemitic canards.[219]

---

seldom fall into it, except lawyers, university men, and men of all sorts that have been bred at Edinburgh' (my italics). B. Franklin, *The Autobiography of Benjamin Franklin*, (Applewood, 2012), p. 17.

[216] A. Gross, 'Vaccination, Inoculation, and Franklin's Grief', U. Haselstein, F. Kelleter, A. Starre, B. Wege, eds., *American Counter/Publics*, (Winter, 2019), pp. 137–158, p. 141.

[217] O. W. Holmes Sr., *Puerperal Fever, as a Private Pestilence*, (Ticknor and Fields, 1855), p. 7.

[218] See the collection of the New South Wales Library, Collection of Ephemera on Health, Box 12: Covid 19, content list https://content-lists.sl.nsw.gov.au/tabular-list/collection-ephemera-health-box-12-covid-19.

[219] European Commission, Directorate-General for Justice and Consumers, M. Comerford, L. Gerster, *The Rise of Antisemitism Online during the Pandemic –*

On this last point, it is crucial to note that 'virality' played a decisive role in the transformation of both antisemitic discourse and pamphleteering from the mid-1930s onwards. While it is true that the equation of 'germs' and 'Jews' had been a staple in nationalist rhetoric since the 1890s, and while 'contagion' had been a prominent trope in the history of antisemitism and anti-Judaism in the early twentieth century,[220] the 1930s saw the publication of a string of enormously popular pamphlets that further radicalized this grim tradition and related it to the spread not only of pathogens, but also of information. Shortly after the momentous publication of his novels *Journey to the End of the Night* (1932) and *Death on Credit* (1936), Louis-Ferdinand Céline, for instance, would publish four antisemitic pamphlets whose brutality remains unmatched in collaborationist literature. Céline, a doctor who had previously been a secretary at the Institute for Hygiene and Epidemiology at the League of Nations, fanatically supported the idea that no distinction between the circulation of discourse, of populations, and of disease should henceforth prevail: science, communism, Jewish men, women, and children, viral pathogens were to be treated as one and the same type of 'infection'[221] of the French body politic. In his explicit calls for the assassination of 320,000 men, women, and children, Céline turned to the pamphlet as the natural vector of antisemitic propaganda.[222]

A Study of French and German Content, (Publications Office of the European Union, 2021), https://data.europa.eu/doi/10.2838/671381.

[220] R. J. Golsan, 'Antisemitism in Modern France: Dreyfus, Vichy, and beyond', A. S. Lindemann, R. S. Levy, eds., *Antisemitism: A History*, (Oxford University Press, 2010), pp. 136–149.

[221] L.-F. Céline, *Mea Culpa & The Life and Work of Semmelweis*, (Sunwise Books, 2020).

[222] I am summarizing arguments I made in: P.-H. Monot, 'On Washing One's Hands of It: Oliver Wendell Holmes, Ignaz Semmelweis, Louis-Ferdinand Céline, and the Cultural Uses of 'Virality'', R. Hölzl, A. Gross, S. Schicktanz, eds., *Narrating Pandemics: Transdisciplinary Approaches to Representations of Communicable Disease*, (University of Toronto Press) forthcoming. See also: R. Tettamanzi, 'Les Pamphlets de Céline et 'l'invasion juive' en médecine', A. Cresciucci, ed., *Actualité de Céline*, (Du Lérot éditeur, 2001), pp. 127–142.

I therefore want to emphasize that the study of polemical literature requires a particularly conscientious attention to the methods and concepts it employs. The popularity of 'virality' is an eminent case in point: it can best be compared to what Hans Blumenberg described as an 'absolute metaphor', that is, a type of figurative language that has become naturalized to such a degree that it is independent from the contents it originally sought to illustrate.[223] Recent and recurrent calls to 'immuniz[e] the public against misinformation'[224] are certainly necessary. Yet on account of the historical origins and political weight of informational 'virality', they make light of two important considerations. First, pamphletary literature does not spread like pathogens. Their material vectors, patterns, and target populations are different: if information did spread across the public sphere in ways resembling to any degree that of pathogens, 'viral' discourse would be endemic and exclude all other kinds of informational circulation. Second, pamphletary publics are neither 'hosts' nor 'passive users' of polemical speech. On the contrary, their agency in selecting, evaluating, and circulating (or not circulating) pamphlets is one of the very few constants in the history of polemical literature since the sixteenth century.[225] Should literary historians and

---

[223] H. Blumenberg, *Paradigms for a Metaphorology*, (Cornell University Press, 2010), p. 4. P.-H. Monot, 'On Washing One's Hands of It: Oliver Wendell Holmes, Ignaz Semmelweis, Louis-Ferdinand Céline, and the Cultural Uses of "Virality"', R. Hölzl, A. Gross, S. Schicktanz, eds., *Narrating Pandemics: Transdisciplinary Approaches to Representations of Communicable Disease*, (University of Toronto Press) forthcoming.

[224] World Health Organization, 'Immunizing the Public against Misinformation' (World Health Organization, 2020). www.who.int/news-room/feature-stories/detail/immunizing-the-public-against-misinformation.

[225] Generally: K. Nahon, J. Hemsley, *Going Viral*, (Polity Press, 2013), pp. 55–81. P.-H. Monot, 'Poor, Nasty, Brutish, and Short: Contemporary Technological Pamphleteering, Popular Literacy, and the Politics of Literary Circulation', in M. Gamper, J. Müller-Tamm, D. Wachter, J. Wrobel, eds., *Der Wert der literarischen Zirkulation / The Value of Literary Circulation*, (Metzler, 2022), pp. 173–185.

book historians willingly dispense with this essential facet of the pamphletary tradition?[226]

6.2 Epilogue: From Pamphleteers to Hashtag Publics?

The 2010s and 2020s arguably provide a negative, yet elegant, answer to this question. These decades have been marked by the increased footprint of digital media on political history, the advent of several pamphletary 'booms' and 'waves', as well as a growing sense of unease regarding marginal, polemical, and accusatory speech and writing. Across Europe and the United States, legislation was passed that facilitated the prosecution of licentious speech, the increase in content moderation, the protection of personal rights, the containment of 'fake news', and the loosening of 'echo chambers', whatever their precise contours and justification may be. Despite this sweeping societal shift, counterpublics have made massive use of digital infrastructures to voice polemical demands in the public and digital spheres, perhaps most visibly within the #MeToo and Black Lives Matter movements, which have employed social media and turned to short-form polemical texts to advance their causes. Online pamphlets, then, are not merely occasions for 'epidemiological encounters'[227] in an 'epidemiological space'[228] among politically passive populations or 'hosts':[229] online pamphlets provide social coalitions with rationally elaborated arguments and a literary-political infrastructure by means of which to exert their agency.

---

[226] I am summarizing arguments I made in: P.-H. Monot, 'On Washing One's Hands of It: Oliver Wendell Holmes, Ignaz Semmelweis, Louis-Ferdinand Céline, and the Cultural Uses of "Virality"', R. Hölzl, A. Gross, S. Schicktanz, eds., *Narrating Pandemics: Transdisciplinary Approaches to Representations of Communicable Disease*, (University of Toronto Press) forthcoming.

[227] T. D. Sampson, *Virality: Contagion Theory in the Age of Networks*, (University of Minnesota Press, 2012), p. 1.

[228] R. L. M. Lee, *The New Collective Behavior in Digital Society: Connection, Contagion, Control*, (Lexington Books, 2023), p. xii.

[229] B. Ghosh, *The Virus Touch: Theorizing Epidemic Media*, (Duke University Press, 2023), p. 54.

Yet scholarship often meets these digital texts with indifference, if not outright condescension. Because they now make increased use of computerized infrastructures of mass publication, social movements online have been variously accused of ushering in 'postfeminism'[230] and 'slacktivism',[231] as well as 'intensify[ing] a lack of connection to real space'.[232] Many accounts of digital activism also point to the 'profound digital dualism'[233] of social media, that is, its growing independence from traditional print media, to explain both the 'viral logic'[234] of networked protest and 'what happens to activist commitment and community-building when the medium used for organising no longer requires sustained face-to-face contact'.[235] Both points ignore the fact that all communication technologies, from the papyrus script to the HTTP protocol, have *always* allowed people to communicate, exchange information, or converse without being physically co-present.[236]

Such dualisms also routinely lead scholarship to disregard the long historicity of polemical literature. Admittedly, the self-assured taxonomies of the early twentieth century fail to grasp the particularities of online pamphleteering (witness Orwell in 1948: 'To ask 'What is a pamphlet?' is rather like asking 'What is a dog?' We all know a dog when we see one'[237]). On the other hand, however, online pamphleteering has insisted on making

[230] S. Dosekun, *Fashioning Postfeminism: Spectacular Femininity and Transnational Culture*, (University of Illinois Press, 2020).

[231] E. Morozov, *Net Delusion: The Dark Side of Internet Freedom*, (Public Affairs, 2011).

[232] T. V. Reed, *The Arts of Protest: Culture and Activism from the Civil Rights Movement to the Present*, (University of Minnesota Press, 2019), p. 330.

[233] Z. Tufekci, *Twitter and Tear Gas: The Power and Fragility of Networked Protest*, (Yale University Press, 2017), p. 130.

[234] J. Sundén, S. Paasonen, *Who's Laughing Now? Feminist Tactics in Social Media*, (MIT Press, 2020), p. 3.

[235] J. Megarry, *The Limitations of Social Media Feminism: No Space of Our Own*, (Palgrave Macmillan, 2020), p. 1.

[236] N. K. Baym, *Personal Connections in the Digital Age*, (Polity Press, 2010), p. 2.

[237] G. Orwell, R. Reynolds, *British Pamphleteers, Volume 1: From the Sixteenth Century to the French Revolution*, (Allan Wingate, 1948), p. 7

its historical filiation known by including clear intertexual references, using the habitual dictions of protest, and conforming to recognizable formal features (Orwell again: 'The true pamphlet, however, is a special literary form which has persisted without radical change for hundreds of years, though it has had its good periods and its bad ones'[238]).

I have argued throughout this Element that we should shift our attention from the physical and formal features of the pamphlet to its social function, that is, to 'what it *does*, how it works within machinic, systemic, and cultural domains'.[239] I would like to conclude on a brief discussion of what this change of perspective allows us to understand – or better understand – of the contours of contemporary online polemic. I want to highlight two important aspects of online pamphleteering: its *addressability* and its *medial hybridity*.

Online pamphlets are 'addressable' in that the current medial infrastructure of polemic (the internet) now enables readers (users) to respond to pamphletary statements *as* implied (and sometimes explicit) addressees, while also affording users a semblance of anonymity. In other words, the proportion of the 'effective' or 'addressable audience'[240] among a quantified total audience has grown exponentially: the dialogical affordances of social media not only encourage, but more importantly make it possible for users to respond to polemical statements 'with substantially diminished transaction costs and monumentally increased circulation'.[241] This 'new structural

---

[238] *Ibid.*, p. 7.

[239] J. Drucker, 'Performative Materiality and Theoretical Approaches to Interface', *Digital Humanities Quarterly*, vol. 7, no. 1 (2013), pp. 1–43, p. 4.

[240] C. Dempster, J. Lee, *The Rise of the Platform Marketer: Performance Marketing with Google, Facebook, and Twitter, Plus the Latest High-Growth Digital Advertising Platforms*, (Wiley, 2015), pp. 1–20.

[241] D. J. Kochan, 'The Blogosphere and The New Pamphleteers', *Nexus*, vol. 11 (2006), pp. 99–109, p. 101. See also Gröppmaier's comments in: S. Gröppmaier, *Textualizing Upheaval: The Pamphletary Politics of Secessionist Movements in the Digital Public Sphere*, (Dissertation, Ludwig-Maximilians-Universität München, 2024), p. 34.

transformation of the public sphere and deliberative politics'[242] has had strong legal implications and has attracted significant attention from scholars of constitutional and civil law. They stress, sometimes with explicit reference to the pamphletary tradition,[243] that anonymous expression online is a right tacitly guaranteed by both the First Amendment of the U.S. Constitution and Article 19 of the Universal Declaration of Human Rights.[244] They also emphasize that freedom of speech and anonymity in turn makes freedom of association not only an enforceable right, but also a practical possibility.[245] By turning to online polemic, counterpublics increasingly perceive their rights to be dependent on infrastructures of communication and association.

The #MeToo movement illustrates this affordance particularly well. From the first posting of the hashtag in October 2017 onwards, the addressability of the campaign was implied in its very title. As the movement took shape on the social media platform Twitter, it called upon users who had been 'sexually harassed or assaulted'[246] to voice their experience *as* explicit addressees. In this way, social media platforms functioned as 'aggregators of knowledge'[247] in a twofold sense: they aggregated polemical, political, or

---

[242] J. Habermas, *A New Structural Transformation of the Public Sphere and Deliberative Politics*, (Polity Press, 2023).

[243] L. Arbatman, J. Villasenor, 'Anonymous Expression and "Unmasking" in Civil and Criminal Proceedings', *Minnesota Journal of Law, Science & Technology*, vol. 23/1 (2022), pp. 78–130, p. 88.

[244] 'Everyone has the right to freedom of opinion and expression; this right includes freedom to hold opinions without interference and to seek, receive and impart information and ideas through any media and regardless of frontiers'. United Nations, *Universal Declaration of Human Rights*, www.un.org/en/about-us/universal-declaration-of-human-rights.

[245] Generally: G. Kateb, 'The Value of Association', A. Gutman, ed., *Freedom of Association*, (Princeton University Press, 1988), pp. 35–63.

[246] Alyssa Milano's original tweet from 15 October 2017 read: 'If you've been sexually harassed or assaulted write "me too" as a reply to this tweet'. It is available here: https://x.com/Alyssa_Milano/status/919659438700670976.

[247] P. Staab, T. Thiel, 'Social Media and the Digital Structural Transformation of the Public Sphere', *Theory, Culture & Society*, vol. 39/4 (2022), pp. 129–143, p. 139.

legal statements ('I was sexually harassed', '#MeToo', 'xyz sexually assaulted me'), *and* they aggregated knowledge about what users knew about one another, thereby undermining *pluralistic ignorance* (i.e., the mistaken belief that others do not share one's knowledge, beliefs, or experiences). This affordance is arguably the crucial feature that sets online pamphleteering apart from its print predecessors. While the latter often circulated widely, they did so confidentially; in effect, readers had no plausible means of assessing the degree to which they belonged to a counterpublic. Online pamphlets, on the contrary, flourish precisely because their circulation is quantified and accompanied by metrics and metadata (i.e., a quantified and communicated number of 'retweets', 'likes', or 'shares'[248]). By circulating online *and* by disclosing the degree to which they do so, pamphletary statements make it plausible for social actors to assume their experience to be common to other actors, thereby mitigating the risks of associating with a (hitherto plausibly minoritarian[249]) counterpublic.[250]

But are tweets 'pamphlets' in any helpful and terminologically consistent sense? The fact that online polemic is increasingly *medially hybrid* is decisive here: most of the polemical 'waves' or 'pamphletary events'[251] of the past decade have had a particularly wide media footprint, at once encompassing print news media, blogs,[252] social media, public events, and more classically 'pamphletary' texts.[253] This hybridization is a recent

---

[248] J. Tormey, 'Pursuing the Digital Pamphleteer', J. Tormey, G. Whitely, eds., *Art, Politics, and the Pamphleteer*, (Bloomsbury Academic, 2021), pp. 347–362, p. 350.

[249] M. Puchner, *Poetry of the Revolution: Marx, Manifestos, and the Avant-Gardes*, (Princeton University Press, 2006), p. 5.

[250] This process was theorized by game theory using the distinction between 'common knowledge' (many users know *x*) and 'mutual knowledge' (many users know *x* and know that other users know *x*). S. Schiffer, *Meaning*, (Clarendon Press, 1972).

[251] See section 5.1.

[252] For a discussion of the pamphletary origins of online blogging, see: J. W. Rettberg, *Blogging*, (Polity Press, 2014), pp. 45–54.

[253] R. O'Mochain, 'The #MeToo Movement in Japan: Tentative Steps towards Transformation', G. Chandra, I. Erlingsdóttir, eds., *The Routledge Handbook of the Politics of the #MeToo Movement*, (Routledge, 2020), pp. 360–371.

development. The #MeToo movement itself started out as an ordinary support network on the social media platform Myspace in 2006.[254] Barely a decade later, the movement could mobilize a wide variety of infrastructural resources and mould them to reflect the movement's polemical intent. In fact, if 2017 could justly be dubbed the 'Year of the Open Letter',[255] it was also the year when a major reconfiguration of the pamphletary tradition became perceptible to most social actors. Open letters to film producer Harvey Weinstein were 'performed' on national television,[256] pamphlets accusing publishers were reprinted and advertised by competing outlets,[257] poems were published, anthologized, and shared on image-based social media platforms,[258] crowdsourced spreadsheets warned of abusive men in the media,[259] polemical texts were read by public figures at the United

[254] Sources pertaining to the foundation of the movement are famously missing. A. Ohlhiser, 'The Woman behind "Me Too" Knew the Power of the Phrase when She Created it – 10 Years Ago', *Washington Post*, October 19, 2017, www.washingtonpost.com/news/the-intersect/wp/2017/10/19/the-woman-behind-me-too-knew-the-power-of-the-phrase-when-she-created-it-10-years-ago/.

[255] E. M. De Wachter, 'Looking Back 2017: The Year of the Open Letter', *Frieze*, 4 December 2017, p. 27. http://web.archive.org/web/20171204175813/https://www.frieze.com/article/looking-back-2017-year-open-letter.

[256] English Playwright Jez Butterworth performed his open letter 'Dear Harvey' on the BBC *Newsnight* program on October 11, 2017. BBC News, 'Playwright Jez Butterworth's Open Letter to Harvey Weinstein', October 12, 2017. www.bbc.co.uk/news/uk-41594764.

[257] Artnet, "We Are Not Surprised': Read the Blistering Open Letter That Art-World Women Wrote About *Artforum*', October 30, 2017. https://news.artnet.com/art-world/not-surprised-read-blistering-open-letter-art-world-women-wrote-artforum-1132463.

[258] D. Alma, *#MeToo: Rallying against Sexual Assault and Harassment: A Women's Poetry Anthology*, (Fair Acre Press, 2018).

[259] The spreadsheet 'Shitty Media Men' was posted in October 2017 via Google's 'Google Sheets' service. J. Peiser, 'Media Men' List Creator Outs Herself, Fearing She Would Be Named', New York Times, 10 January 2018. www.nytimes.com/2018/01/10/business/media/a-feminist-twitter-campaign-targets-harpers-magazine-and-katie-roiphe.html?_r=0.

Nations Headquarters,[260] and a set of secondary polemics incriminated institutions of higher education in the most refined of scholastic tones.[261] In short, the shift away from pamphleteering as a literary format to pamphleteering as a broader social activity was no longer merely a theoretical proposition, but a collective practice wholly independent from the original print infrastructure of short-form dissent.

To put it differently, and perhaps more prudently, pamphleteering now appears to be an increasingly legitimate activity for demographics which have access to an ever-growing range of media infrastructures and institutional contexts. There is, of course, an obvious quantitative reason for this: women represent half of the world's population. As such, the growing digital footprint of polemical styles represents a crucial shift in democratic cultures.

---

[260] S. Miller, 'United Nations Commission on the Status of Women', 16 March 2018. https://media.un.org/unifeed/en/asset/d211/d2111891.

[261] See for instance the intense controversy around the adequation of transgender and transracial identity. R. Tuvel, 'In Defense of Transracialism', *Hypatia: A Journal of Feminist Philosophy*, vol. 32/2 (Spring 2017), pp. 263–278.

Bibliography

Adams, T. R., N. Barker, 'A New Model for the Study of the Book', in N. Barker, ed., *A Potencie of Life: Books in Society: The Clark Lectures 1986–1987*, (The British Library, 1993), pp. 5–43.

Adut, A., *On Scandal: Moral Disturbances in Society, Politics, and Art*, (Cambridge University Press, 2009).

Alma, D., *#MeToo: Rallying against Sexual Assault and Harassment: A Women's Poetry Anthology*, (Fair Acre Press, 2018).

Anaya, S. J., *Indigenous Peoples in International Law*, (Oxford University Press, 2007).

Anonymous, 'The Eloquent Peasant', in M. Lichtheim, ed., *Ancient Egyptian Literature*, (University of California Press, 2019), pp. 214–292.

Anonymous, 'Alternatives', *Women's Voices*, Vol. 1, No. 1 (1974), p. 17. https://content.wisconsinhistory.org/digital/collection/p15932coll8/id/36388/rec/2.

Anonymous, 'Army Uses Scare Tactics against WACs', *Bragg Briefs*, Vol. 4, No. 4 (May 1971), p. 6. www.jstor.org/stable/community.28034433.

Anonymous, 'Clip This to Save Your Life', in *Up against the Bulkhead*, Vol. 2, No. 3, Issue 8 (June 1971), p. 1. https://content.wisconsinhistory.org/digital/collection/p15932coll8/id/89802.

Anonymous, 'Editorial Policy', *Fun Travel Adventure*, Vol. 1 (23 June 1968), pp. 1–2. https://content.wisconsinhistory.org/digital/collection/p15932coll8/id/42075.

Anonymous, 'Editor's Statement', *Voice of the Lumpen*, Vol. 1/4 (1971), p. 8. www.jstor.org/stable/community.28046313.

Anonymous, 'GIs & Workers Fight Racism', *Highway 13*, Vol. 1, No. 6 (July–August 1873), pp. 1–10. www.jstor.org/stable/pdf/community.28038376.pdf.

Anonymous, 'Operation Awareness Is Dying', *Bragg Briefs*, Vol. 4, No. 5 (June 1971), p. 1. www.jstor.org/stable/community.28034435.

Anonymous, 'Our Bodies, Ourselves', *Women's Voices*, Vol. 1, No. 1 (1974), p. 4.

Anonymous, 'Self Help', *Women's Voices*, Vol. 1, No. 1 (1974), pp. 11–12. https://content.wisconsinhistory.org/digital/collection/p15932coll8/id/36382/rec/2.

Anonymous, 'Voice of the Lumpen Manifesto', *Voice of the Lumpen*, Vol. 1 (1971), p. 1. www.jstor.org/stable/community.28046308.

Arbatman, L., J. Villasenor, 'Anonymous Expression and "Unmasking" in Civil and Criminal Proceedings', *Minnesota Journal of Law, Science & Technology*, Vol. 23/1 (2022), pp. 78–130.

Arruzza, C., T. Bhattacharya, N. Fraser, *Feminism for the 99%: A Manifesto*, (Verso, 2019).

Artnet, '"We Are Not Surprised": Read the Blistering Open Letter That Art-World Women Wrote about *Artforum*', 30 October 2017. https://news.artnet.com/art-world/not-surprised-read-blistering-open-letter-art-world-women-wrote-artforum-1132463.

Auspitz, K., *The Radical Bourgeoisie: The Ligue de l'Enseignement Supérieur and the origins of the Third Republic, 1866–1885*, (Cambridge University Press, 2002).

Baker, S., *Surrealism, History, and Revolution*, (Peter Lang, 2003).

Banks, D., R. Erdoes, *Ojibwa Warrior: Dennis Banks and the Rise of the American Indian Movement*, (University of Oklahoma Press, 2004).

Basart, S., *Les Éditions Jules Rouff (1877–1912): Monographie d'un éditeur populaire*, (Université de Saint Quentin en Yvelines, 1994).

Baym, N. K., *Personal Connections in the Digital Age*, (Polity Press, 2010).

BBC News, 'Playwright Jez Butterworth's Open Letter to Harvey Weinstein', 12 October 2017. www.bbc.co.uk/news/uk-41594764.

Bebnowski, D., 'Pressing Social Orders', in P.-H. Monot, D. Bebnowski, S. Gröppmaier, eds., *Activist Writing: History, Politics, Rhetoric*, (intercom, 2024), pp. 115–127.

Bebnowski, D., 'Radikaler Druck – Druckerzeugnisse und Radikalitäten in der zweiten Welle des Feminismus in den USA'. *Österreichische Zeitschrift für Geschichtswissenschaften*, Vol. 35, No. 1 (2024), pp. 70–95.

Beins, A., *Liberation in Print: Feminist Periodicals and Social Movement Identity*, (University of Georgia Press, 2017).

Bellenger, Y., 'Le pamphlet avant le pamphlet: le mot et la chose', *Cahiers de l'Association International des Études Françaises*, 36 (1984), pp. 87–96.

Blumenberg, H., *Paradigms for a Metaphorology*, (Cornell University Press, 2010).

Blurton, H., *Inventing William of Norwich: Thomas of Monmouth, Antisemitism, and Literary Culture, 1150–1200*, (University of Pennsylvania Press, 2022).

Boltanski, L., *On Critique: A Sociology of Emancipation*, (Polity Press, 2011).

Boltanksi, L., E. Chiapello, *The New Spirit of Capitalism*, (Verso, 2007).

Bourdieu, P., *The Rules of Art: Genesis and Structure of the Literary Field*, (Stanford University Press, 1995).

Bréville, B., 'Pétitionnaires de tous les pays … ', *Le Monde diplomatique* (August 2020), p. 28.

Burgdorf, W., 'Der intergouvernementale publizistische Diskurs. Agitation und Emanzipation, politische Gelegenheitsschriften und ihre Bedeutung für die Entstehung politischer Öffentlichkeit im Alten Reich', in J. Arndt, E.-B. Körber, eds., *Das Mediensystem im Alten Reich der Frühen Neuzeit (1600–1750)*, (Vandenhoeck & Ruprecht, 2010), pp. 75–98.

Bürger, P., *Theory of the Avant-Garde*, (Manchester University Press, 1984).

Burke, K., *A Grammar of Motives*, (Prentice-Hall, 1945).

Burrows, S., 'French Censorship on the Eve of the Revolution', in N. Moore, ed., *Censorship and the Limits of the Literary: A Global View*, (Bloomsbury, 2017), pp. 13–32.

Castoriadis, C., *The Imaginary Institution of Society*, (MIT Press, 1987).

Castronovo, A., 'A Superfood Manifesto', *Blast Magazine*, 23 June 2011, https://blastmagazine.com/2011/06/23/a-superfood-manifesto/.

Caws, M. A., 'The Poetics of the Manifesto: Nowness and Newness', in M. A. Caws, ed., *Manifesto: A Century of Isms*, (University of Nebraska Press, 2001), pp. xix–xxxi.

Céline, L.-F., *Mea Culpa & the Life and Work of Semmelweis*, (Sunwise Books, 2020).

Cetre, N., *L'édition en fascicules de romans français entre 1870 et 1914 et leur conservation par la BnF*, (Ecole Nationale Supérieure des Sciences de l'Information et des Bibliothèques, 2002).

Chartier, A. M., *L'école et la lecture obligatoire: Histoire et paradoxes des pratiques d'enseignement de la lecture*, (Retz, 2015).

Cohn, M., K. Gilberd, *Rules of Disengagement: The Politics and Honor of Military Dissent*, (New York University Press, 2009).

Crain, P., 'New Histories of Literacy', in S. Eliot, J. Rose, eds., *A Companion to the History of the Book*, vol. 1, (Wiley, 2019), pp. 143–156.

Currin, S. W. Jr., *An Army of the Willing: Fayette'Nam, Soldier Dissent, and the Untold Story of the All-Volunteer Force*, (Dissertation, Duke University, 2015). https://dukespace.lib.duke.edu/server/api/core/bit streams/8cbcdadb-75f5-4588-9bfa-184adb926743/content.

Darnton, R., *Poetry and the Police: Communication Networks in Eighteenth-Century Paris*, (Belknap Press, 2010).

Darnton, R., *The Literary Underground of the Old Regime*, (Harvard University Press, 1982).

Darnton, R., 'What Is the History of Books?', *Daedalus*, Vol. 111, No. 3, (1982), pp. 65–83.

Dartigues, L., 'Une généalogie de *l'intellectuel spécifique*', *Astérion*, Vol. 12 (2014), pp. 1–16.

David, A., 'The *nmḥ* and the Paradox of the Voiceless in *The Eloquent Peasant*', *The Journal of Egyptian Archeology*, Vol. 97 (2011), pp. 73–85.

Davis, H. V., 'The High-tech Lynching and the High-tech Overseer: Thoughts from the Anita Hill/Clarence Thomas Affair', *The Black Scholar*, Vol. 22, No. 1/2, (Winter 1991–Spring 1992), pp. 27–29.

De Wachter, E. M., 'Looking Back 2017: The Year of the Open Letter', *Frieze*, 4 December 2017, p. 27. http://web.archive.org/web/20171204175813/https://www.frieze.com/article/looking-back-2017-year-open-letter.

Deicke, A. J. E., 'Networks of Conflict: Analyzing the "Culture of Controversy" in Polemical Pamphlets of Intra-Protestant Disputes (1548–1580)', *Journal of Historical Network Research*, Vol. 1 (2017), pp. 71–105.

Deloria, V. Jr., *Behind the Trail of Broken Treaties: An Indian Declaration of Independence*, (University of Texas Press, 1984).

Dempster, C., J. Lee, *The Rise of the Platform Marketer: Performance Marketing with Google, Facebook, and Twitter, Plus the Latest High-Growth Digital Advertising Platforms*, (Wiley, 2015).

Dentzel, Z., D. Ek, K. Hed, et al., *Startup Manifesto: A Manifesto for Entrepreneurship & Innovation to Power Growth in the EU*, www.startupmanifesto.eu/#manifesto.

Department of Defense, *Department of Defense Appropriations for 1972, Hearings before a Subcommittee of the Committee on Appropriations*, Part 4: *Operation and Maintenance*, (U.S. Government Printing Office, 1971), p. 819.

Deseriis, M., 'On the Symbolic Power of Shared Pseudonyms', *Seachange*, Vol. 6, No. 1 (2015), pp. 51–62.

Dosekun, S., *Fashioning Postfeminism: Spectacular Femininity and Transnational Culture*, (University of Illinois Press, 2020).

Drake, D., *French Intellectuals and Politics from the Dreyfus Affair to the Occupation*, (Palgrave Macmillan, 2005).

Drucker, J., 'Performative Materiality and Theoretical Approaches to Interface', *Digital Humanities Quarterly*, Vol. 7, No. 1 (2013), pp. 1–43.

Eberly, R. A., *Citizen Critics: Literary Public Spheres*, (University of Illinois Press, 2000).

Ebert, T. L., 'Manifesto as Theory and Theory as Material Force: Toward a Red Polemic', *JAC*, Vol. 23, No. 3 (2003), pp. 553–562.

Eisenstein, E. L., *Divine Art, Infernal Machine: The Reception of Printing in the West from First Impressions to the Sense of an Ending*, (University of Pennsylvania Press, 2011).

Eisenstein, E. L., *The Printing Press as an Agent of Change: Communications and Cultural Transformations in Early-Modern Europe*, (Cambridge University Press, 1997).

Elinson, E., 'Sailors are Just Cogs in the Bombing Machine: Two Coral Sea Sailors Ashore', *Liberation News Service*, Vol. 416, No. 4 (March 1972), p. 1. https://content.wisconsinhistory.org/digital/collection/p15932coll8/id/72983.

Engle, K., *The Elusive Promise of Indigenous Development: Rights, Culture, Strategy*, (Duke University Press, 2010).

European Commission, Directorate-General for Justice and Consumers, M. Comerford, L. Gerster, *The Rise of Antisemitism Online during the Pandemic – A Study of French and German Content*, (Publications Office of the European Union, 2021), https://data.europa.eu/doi/10.2838/671381.

Executive Services Directorate, 'Department of Defense Directive 1325.6', Washington, 7 September 1969.

Federal Bureau of Investigation Memorandum on the American Indian Movement calling for the implementation of an informant development program, 27 November 1972, Federal Bureau of Investigation Library.

Ferguson, R. A., *Reading the Early Republic*, (Harvard University Press, 2004).

Flannery, K. T., *Feminist Literacies, 1968–1975*, (University of Illinois Press, 2005).

Franklin, B., *The Autobiography of Benjamin Franklin*, (Applewood, 2012).

Frischmann, B., 'Privatization and Commercialization of the Internet Infrastructure: Rethinking Market Intervention into Government and Government Intervention into the Market', *Columbia Science and Technology Law Review*, Vol. 2 (2001), pp. 1–70. www.columbia.edu/cu/stlr/html/volume2/frischmann.pdf.

Galchinsky, M., 'Political Pamphlet', in F. Burwick, ed., *The Encyclopedia of Romantic Literature*, Vol. 2, (Wiley-Blackwell, 2012), pp. 1025–1034.

Gaver, W. H., 'Technological Affordances', *Proceedings of CHI'91*, (New Orleans, Louisiana, 28 April–2 May 1991), ACM, New York, pp. 79–84.

Ghosh, B., *The Virus Touch: Theorizing Epidemic Media*, (Duke University Press, 2023).

Ghosh, K., *The Wycliffite Heresies: Authority and the Interpretation of Texts*, (Cambridge University Press, 2004).

Golsan, R. J., 'Antisemitism in Modern France: Dreyfus, Vichy, and beyond', A. S. Lindemann, R. S. Levy, eds., *Antisemitism: A History*, (Oxford University Press, 2010), pp. 136–149.

Gröppmaier, S., *Textualizing Upheaval: The Pamphletary Politics of Secessionist Movements in the Digital Public Sphere*, (Dissertation, Ludwig-Maximilians-Universität München, 2024).

Gross, A., 'Vaccination, Inoculation, and Franklin's Grief', U. Haselstein, F. Kelleter, A. Starre, B. Wege, eds., *American Counter/Publics*, (Winter, 2019), pp. 137–158.

Habermas, J., *A New Structural Transformation of the Public Sphere and Deliberative Politics*, (Polity Press, 2023).

Habermas, J., *The Structural Transformation of the Public Sphere: An Inquiry into a Category of Bourgeois Society*, (MIT Press, 1991).

Halasz, A., *The Marketplace of Print: Pamphlets and the Public Sphere in Early Modern England*, (Cambridge University Press, 1997).

Hansen, C., *A Daoist Theory of Chinese Thought: A Philosophical Interpretation*, (Oxford University Press, 1992).

Hartman, A., *A War for the Soul of America: A History of the Culture Wars*, (Chicago University Press, 2019).

Hasenbank, A., 'Formal Protest: Reconsidering the Poetics of Canadian Pamphleteering', B. Vautour, E. Wunker, T. V. Mason, C. Verduyn, eds., *Public Poetics: Critical Issues in Canadian Poetry and Poetics*, (Wilfrid Laurier University Press, 2015), pp. 231–252.

Hastings, M., C. Passard, J. Rennes, 'Les mutations du pamphlet dans la France contemporaine', *Mots: Les langages du politique* 91 (2009), pp. 5–17.

Helmreich, S., *A Book of Waves*, (Duke University Press, 2023).

Heng, G., *The Global Middle Ages: An Introduction*, (Cambridge University Press, 2021).

Hersford, V., *Feeling Women's Liberation*, (Duke University Press, 2013).

Hirschman, A. O., 'Opinionated Opinions and Democracy', in J. Adelman, ed., *The Essential Hirschman*, (Princeton University Press, 2013), pp. 284–292.

Höhn, M., 'The Black Panther Solidarity Committees and the Voice of the Lumpen', *German Studies Review*, Vol. 31, No. 1 (February 2008), pp. 133–154.

Hollander, J den, H. Paul, R. Peters, 'Introduction: The Metaphor of Historical Distance', *History and Theory*, Vol. 50, No. 4 (December 2011), pp. 1–10.

Holmes, O. W., Sr., *Puerperal Fever, as a Private Pestilence*, (Ticknor and Fields, 1855).

Holstun, J., 'Introduction', in J. Holstun, ed., *Pamphlet Wars: Prose in the English Revolution*, (Frank Cass, 1992), pp. 1–13.

Houghton, R., A. O'Donoghue, 'Manifestos as Constituent Power: Performing a Feminist Revolution', *Global Constitutionalism*, Vol. 12, No. 3 (2023), pp. 412–437.

Huelsenbeck, R., *En Avant Dada*, in R. Motherwell, ed., *The Dada Painters and Poets: An Anthology*, (Harvard University Press, 1981), pp. 21–48.

International Section of the Black Panther Party, Revolutionary Peoples Communications Network, 'what Is the Revolutionary Peoples Communications Network', *Voice of the Lumpen*, Vol. 1, No. 8 (October 1971), p. 2.

Janus, K. K., 'Finding Common Feminist Ground: The Role of the Next Generation in Shaping Feminist Legal Theory', *Duke Journal of Gender Law & Policy*, Vol. 20, No. 255 (2013), pp. 255–285.

Jarvis, J., *The Gutenberg Parenthesis: The Age of Print and its Lessons for the Age of the Internet*, (Bloomsbury Academic, 2023).

John, P. O., *Publishing in Paris, 1570–1590: A Bibliometric Analysis*, (Ph.D., University of St Andrews, 2010).

Johnson, L. B., SAC Letter 67–70, 28 November 1967. https://ia601007.us.archive.org/14/items/FBIRabbleRouserAgitatorIndexHQ1577782Sections14/FBI%20Rabble%20Rouser-Agitator%20Index%20-%20HQ%20157–7782%2C%20sections%201–4.pdf.

Johnson, L. B., SAC Letter 67–47, 4 April 1967,

Johnson, T. R., *The Occupation of Alcatraz Island: Indian Self-determination and the Rise of Indian Activism*, (University of Illinois Press, 1996).

Jones-Katz, G. ed., 'Huey P. Newton and Bobby Seale: What We Want Now!, What We Believe: The Black Panther Party Ten-Point Platform and Program', in P.-H. Monot, ed., *The Arts of Autonomy: A Living Anthology of Polemical Literature*, (The Arts of Autonomy, 2022), pp. 1–19.

Josephy, A. M. Jr., J. Nagel, T. Johnson, eds., *Red Power: The American Indians' Fight for Freedom*, (University of Nebraska Press, 1999).

Junker, C., 'Claiming Class: The Manifesto between Categorical Disruption and Stabilisation', *Culture, Theory and Critique*, Vol. 63, No. 2–3, (2023), pp. 189–205.

Kateb, G., 'The Value of Association', A. Gutman, ed., *Freedom of Association*, (Princeton University Press, 1988), pp. 35–63.

Kieserling, A., *Kommunikation unter Anwesenden: Studien über Interaktionssysteme*, (Suhrkamp, 1999).

Knights, M., *Representation and Misrepresentation in Later Stuart Britain: Partisanship and Political Culture*, (Oxford University Press, 2006).

Kochan, D. J., 'The Blogosphere and the New Pamphleteers', *Nexus*, Vol. 11 (2006), pp. 99–109.

Kouvelakis, S., *Philosophy and Revolution: From Kant to Marx*, (Verso, 2018).

Kramer, D. W. ed., *Johann Tetzel's Rebuttal against Luther's Sermon on Indulgences and Grace*, (Pitts Theology Library, 2012).

Kremmel, S., 'Born Translated Manifesto', in P.-H. Monot, D. Bebnowski, S. Gröppmaier, eds., *Activist Writing: History, Politics, Rhetoric*, (Intercom, 2024), pp. 98–111.

Lee, R. L. M., *The New Collective Behavior in Digital Society: Connection, Contagion, Control*, (Lexington Books, 2023).

Lennon, R. E., *Wedded Wife: A Feminist History of Marriage*, (Quarto, 2023).

Leppin, V., T. J. Wengert, 'Sources for and against the Posting of the Ninety-Five Theses', *Lutheran Quarterly*, Vol. 29 (2015), pp. 373–398.

Leroy, G., 'Je pars, soldat de la République', in G. Leroy, ed., *Charles Péguy: L'inclassable*, (Armand Colin, 2014), pp. 291–296.

Levine, C., *Forms: Whole, Rhythm, Hierarchy, Network*, (Princeton University Press, 2015).

Lewes, J., *Protest and Survive: Underground GI Newspapers during the Vietnam War*, (Praeger, 2003).

Linfield, M., *Freedom under Fire: U.S. Civil Liberties in Times of War*, (South End Press, 1990).

Lockridge, K. A., *Literacy in Colonial New England: An Enquiry into the Social Context of Literacy in the Early Modern West*, (Norton, 1974).

Lordon, F., 'La paille et la poutre', *Le Monde diplomatique*, 24.08.2012, https://blog.mondediplo.net/2012-08-24-Conspirationnisme-la-paille-et-la-poutre.

Loughran, T., *The Republic in Print: Print Culture in the Age of U.S. Nation Building, 1770–1870*, (Columbia University Press, 2007).

Lucks, D. S., *Selma to Saigon: The Civil Rights Movement and the Vietnam War*, (University Press of Kentucky, 2014).

Luhmann, N., *Social Systems*, (Stanford University Press, 1995).

Luther, M., 'The Ninety-Five Theses: A Disputation to Clarify the Power of Indulgences', in W. R. Russell, ed., *The Ninety-Five Theses and Other Writings*, (Penguin, 2017), pp. 1–13.

Marling, W., *Gatekeepers: The Emergence of World Literature & the 1960s*, (Oxford University Press, 2016).

Marquis de Sade, 'Philosophy in the Bedroom', in R. Seaver, A. Wainhouse, eds., *Justine, Philosophy in the Bedroom, and Other Writings*, (Grove Press, 1965), pp. 179–367.

McCammon, H. J., M. Moon, 'Social Movement Coalitions', in D. Della Porta, M. Diani, eds., *The Oxford Handbook of Social Movements*, (Oxford University Press, 2015), pp. 326–339.

McCleery, A., 'The Paperback Evolution: Tauchnitz, Albatross and Penguin', in N. Matthews, N. Moody, eds., *Judging a Book by its Cover: Fans, Publishers, Designers and the Marketing of Fiction*, (Ashgate, 2007), pp. 3–18.

McDowell, D. E., 'Telling Slavery in "Freedom's" Time: Post-Reconstruction and the Harlem Renaissance', in A. Fisch, ed., *The Cambridge Companion to the African American Slave Narrative*, (Cambridge University Press, 2007), pp. 150–167.

McGann, J., *The Textual Condition*, (Princeton University Press, 1991).

McKenzie, D. F., *Bibliography and the Sociology of Texts*, (Cambridge University Press, 2004).

McStay, A., *Creativity and Advertising: Affect, Events and Process*, (Routledge, 2013).

Megarry, J., *The Limitations of Social Media Feminism: No Space of Our Own*, (Palgrave Macmillan, 2020).

Miller, S., 'United Nations Commission on the Status of Women', 16 March 2018. https://media.un.org/unifeed/en/asset/d211/d2111891.

Mo Zi, *The Book of Master Mo*, I. Johnston, ed., (Penguin, 2013).

Monaghan, E. J., *Learning to Read and Write in Colonial America*, (University of Massachusetts Press, 2005).

Monot, P.-H. ed., 'Aristophanes: *The Clouds*. A Commented Edition with Contextual Sources, Translated by Ian Johnston' (Version 1.0), in P.-H. Monot, ed., *The Arts of Autonomy: A Living Anthology of Polemical Literature*, (The Arts of Autonomy, 2024), pp. 1–121.

Monot, P.-H., 'Art, Autonomy, Philology: Project Parameters', in P.-H. Monot, D. Bebnowski, S. Gröppmaier, eds., *Activist Writing: History, Politics, Rhetoric*, (Intercom, 2024), pp. 16–23.

Monot, P.-H., 'Émile Zola: 'J'accuse . . . ! ': A Commented Bilingual Edition, Including Contextual Sources and a Facsimile Copy of Émile Zola's Manuscript', in P.-H. Monot, ed., *The Arts of Autonomy: A Living Anthology of Polemical Literature*, (The Arts of Autonomy, 2022), pp. 1–91.

Monot, P.-H., 'Kill Lists: Ideas of Order in the Pamphlet', *KWI Blog*, (20 April 2022), https://doi.org/10.37189/kwi-blog/20220420-0830.

Monot, P.-H., 'On Washing One's Hands of It: Oliver Wendell Holmes, Ignaz Semmelweis, Louis-Ferdinand Céline, and the Cultural Uses of "Virality"', in R. Hölzl, A. Gross, S. Schicktanz, eds., *Narrating Pandemics: Transdisciplinary Approaches to Representations of Communicable Disease*, (University of Toronto Press), forthcoming.

Monot, P.-H., 'Poor, Nasty, British, and Short. Contemporary Pamphleteering, Popular Literacy, and the Politics of Literary Circulation', in M. Gamper, J. Müller-Tamm, D. Wachter, J. Wrobel, eds., *Der Wert der literarischen Zirkulation / The Value of Literary Circulation*, (Springer, 2023), pp. 173–185.

Monot, P.-H., 'Pretty Pamphlets', in P.-H. Monot, D. Bebnowski, S. Gröppmaier, eds., *Activist Writing: History, Politics, Rhetoric*, (Intercom, 2024), pp. 68–82.

Monot, P.-H. ed., 'Queers Read This: The Queer Nation Manifesto: A Commented Edition with Contextual Sources and a Facsimile Copy of the Original Pamphlet' (Version 1.0), in P.-H. Monot, ed., *The Arts of Autonomy: A Living Anthology of Polemical Literature*, (The Arts of Autonomy, 2024), pp. 1–32. https://artsautonomy.hypotheses.org.

Monot, P.-H. ed., 'The Book of Mozi: Chapter 39. "Against the Confucians" (Fei Ru Xia). A Commented Edition with Contextual Sources' (Version 1.0), in P.-H. Monot, ed., *The Arts of Autonomy: A Living Anthology of Polemical Literature*, (The Arts of Autonomy, 2022), pp. 1–18.

Monot, P.-H. ed. '*The Trail of Broken Treaties 20-Point Position Paper: An Indian Manifesto*. A Commented Edition with Contextual Sources' (Version 1.0), P.-H. Monot, ed., *The Arts of Autonomy: A Living Anthology of Polemical Literature*, (The Arts of Autonomy, 2022), pp. 1–46. https://artsautonomy.hypotheses.org.

Morozov, E. *Net Delusion: The Dark Side of Internet Freedom*, (Public Affairs, 2011).

Mouffe, C. *The Return of the Political*, (Verso, 1993).

Nahon, K., J. Hemsley, *Going Viral*, (Polity Press, 2013).

Negt, O., A. Kluge, *Öffentlichkeit und Erfahrung: Zur Organisationsanalyse von bürgerlicher und proletarischer Öffentlichkeit*, (Suhrkamp 1973).

Ober, J., *The Rise and Fall of Classical Greece*, (Princeton University Press, 2015).

Ohlheiser, A., 'The Woman behind "Me Too" Knew the Power of the Phrase when She Created It – 10 Years Ago', *Washington Post*, 19 October 2017. www.washingtonpost.com/news/the-intersect/wp/2017/10/19/the-woman-behind-me-too-knew-the-power-of-the-phrase-when-she-created-it-10-years-ago/.

Olson, M., *The Logic of Collective Action*, (Harvard University Press, 2002).

O'Mochain, R., 'The #MeToo Movement in Japan: Tentative Steps towards Transformation', G. Chandra, I. Erlingsdóttir, eds., *The Routledge Handbook of the Politics of the #MeToo Movement*, (Routledge, 2020), pp. 360–371.

Orwell, G., 'Introduction', G. Orwell, R. Reynolds, eds., *British Pamphleteers. Volume 1, From the Sixteenth Century to the French Revolution*, (London: Allan Wingate, 1948), pp. 7–17.

Paine, T., 'Common Sense', in J. M. Opal, ed., *Common Sense and Other Writings*, (Norton, 2012), pp. 3–38.

Painter, C., P. Ferrucci, '"Ask What You Can Do to the Army": A Textual Analysis of the Underground GI Press during the Vietnam War', *Media, War & Conflict*, Vol. 12, No. 3 (September 2019), pp. 354–367.

Pearce, K. C., 'The Radical Feminist Manifesto as Generic Appropriation: Gender, Genre, and Second Wave Resistance', *Southern Journal of Communication*, Vol. 64, No.4 (1999), pp. 307–315.

Péguy, C., *L'Argent*, (Gallimard, 1932).

Péret, B., *Je ne mange pas de ce pain-là*, (Syllepse, 2010).

Perloff, M., *The Futurist Moment: Avant-Garde, Avant Guerre, and the Language of Rupture*, (University of Chicago Press, 1982).

Pettegree, A., 'Books, Pamphlets and Polemic', A. Pettegree, ed., *The Reformation World*, (Routledge, 2000), pp. 109–126, p. 110.

Pettegree, A., *Brand Luther: How an Unheralded Monk Turned His Small Town Into a Center of Publishing, Made Himself the Most Famous Man in Europe – and Started the Protestant Reformation*, (Penguin, 2015).

Pettegree, A. ed., *Broadsheets: Single-Sheet Publishing in the First Age of Print*, (Brill, 2017).

Pettegree, A., *The French Book and the European Book World*, (Brill, 2007).

Private Cornell Rifleman, 'A better way', *ACT*, Vol. 1, No. 1 (1967), p. 1. https://content.wisconsinhistory.org/digital/collection/p15932coll8/id/9797/rec/1.

Puchner, M., *Poetry of the Revolution: Marx, Manifestos, and the Avant-Gardes*, (Princeton University Press, 2006).

Raymond, J., *Pamphlets and Pamphleteering in Early Modern Britain*, (Cambridge University Press, 2003).

Reckwitz, A., *Das hybride Subjekt: Eine Theorie der Subjektkulturen von der bürgerlichen Moderne zur Postmoderne*, (Suhrkamp, 2020).

Reed, T. V., *The Arts of Protest: Culture and Activism from the Civil Rights Movement to the Present*, (University of Minnesota Press, 2019).

Rettberg, J. W., *Blogging*, (Polity Press, 2014).

Rex, R., *The Making of Martin Luther*, (Princeton University Press, 2017).

Rifkin, J., *The Age of Access: The New Culture of Hypercapitalism*, (Penguin, 2001).

Rigby, S. H., *English Society in the Later Middle Ages: Class, Status, Gender*, (Macmillan, 1995).

Rips, G., 'The Campaign against the Underground Press', in A. Janowitz, N. A. Peters, eds., *Unamerican Activities: Pen American Center Report*, (City Lights Bookstore, 1981), pp. 37–158.

Rosen, R. M., 'Performance and Textuality in Aristophanes' Clouds', *The Yale Journal of Criticism*, Vol. 10, No.2 (1997), pp. 397–421.

Rosenfeld, S., *Subversives: The FBI's War on Student Radicals, and Reagan's Rise to Power*, (Farrar, Straus, and Giroux, 2012).

Rowley, M. V., 'The Idea of Ancestry: Of Feminist Genealogies and Many Other Things', C. McCann, S. Kim, eds., *Feminist Theory Reader: Local and Global Perspectives*, (Routledge, 2016), pp. 77–83.

Sampson, T. D., *Virality: Contagion Theory in the Age of Networks*, (University of Minnesota Press, 2012).

Sarachild, K., 'A Program for Feminist "Consciousness Raising"', in S. Firestone, A. Koedt, eds., *Notes from the Second Year: Women's Liberation: Major Writings of the Radical Feminists*, (Radical Feminism, 1970), pp. 78–80.

Sayer, J. W., *Ghost Dancing the Law: The Wounded Knee Trials*, (Harvard University Press, 1997).

Schiffer, S., *Meaning*, (Clarendon Press, 1972).

Schilling, J., 'Einleitung', in M. Luther, J. Schilling, ed., *Christusglaube und Rechfertigung*, (Evangelische Verlagsanstalt, 2006), pp. ix–xxxix.

Scott, B. R., *Capitalism: Its Origins and Evolution as a System of Governance*, (Springer, 2011).

Schmalstieg, M., B. Crevits, V. Kruug, eds., *Manifestos for the Internet Age*, (sine loco, 2016).

Seidman, D., 'Paper Soldiers: The *Ally* and the GI Underground Press during the Vietnam War', J. L. Baughman, J. Ratner-Rosenhagen, J. P. Dansky, eds., *Protest on the Page: Essays on Print and the Culture of Dissent Since 1865*, (The University of Wisconsin Press, 2015), pp. 183–202.

Shanley, M. L., *Feminism, Marriage, and the Law in Victorian England*, (Princeton University Press, 1989).

Shupak, N., 'A New Source for the Study of the Judiciary and Law of Ancient Egypt: "The Tale of the Eloquent Peasant"', *Journal of near Eastern Studies*, Vol. 51, No.1 (January 1992), pp. 1–18.

Simmons, C., *Making Marriage Modern: Women's Sexuality from the Progressive Era to World War II*, (Oxford University Press, 2009).

Solanas, V., *S.C.U.M. (Society for Cutting up Men) Manifesto*, (Olympia Press, 1967).

Staab, P., T. Thiel, 'Social Media and the Digital Structural Transformation of the Public Sphere', *Theory, Culture & Society*, Vol. 39, No.4 (2022), pp. 129–143.

Stallybrass, P., '"Little Jobs": Broadsides and the Printing Revolution', S. A. Baron, E. N. Lindqvist, E. F. Shevlin, eds., *Agent of Change: Print Culture Studies after Elizabeth L. Eisenstein*, (University of Massachusetts Press, 2007), pp. 315–341.

Stallybrass, P., 'Everyday Objects', in J. Symonds, ed., *A Cultural History of Objects in the Renaissance*, (Bloomsbury Academic, 2021), pp. 103–124.

Strayer, J. R., *On the Medieval Origins of the Modern State*, (Princeton University Press, 2005).

Studer, B., *Travellers of the World Revolution: A Global History of the Communist International*, (Verso, 2023).

Sundén, J., S. Paasonen, *Who's Laughing Now? Feminist Tactics in Social Media*, (MIT Press, 2020).

Tetrault, L., *The Myth of Seneca Falls: Memory and the Women's Suffrage Movement, 1848–1898*, (The University of North Carolina Press, 2014).

Tettamanzi, R., 'Les Pamphlets de Céline et 'l'invasion juive' en médecine'', A. Cresciucci, ed., *Actualité de Céline*, (Du Lérot éditeur, 2001), pp. 127–142.

Thoburn, N., 'Communist Objects and the Values of Printed Matter', *Social Text*, Vol. 28/2, No. 103 (Summer 2010), pp. 1–30.

Thompson, B., 'Multiracial Feminism: Recasting the Chronology of Second Wave Feminism', *Feminist Studies*, Summer, Vol. 28, No. 2 (2002), pp. 336–360.

Thumala Olave, M. A. ed., *The Cultural Sociology of Reading: The Meanings of Reading and Books across the World*, (Palgrave Macmillan, 2022).

Tierney, J., 'Throngs Cheer at Gay and Lesbian March', *New York Times*, 25 June 1990, section B, page 1.

Tischler, B., 'Breaking Ranks: GI Antiwar Newspapers and the Culture of Protest', *Vietnam Generation*, Vol. 2, No. 1, Article 4, pp. 20–50.

Tolan, J. V., *Saracens: Islam in the Medieval European Imagination*, (Columbia University Press, 2002).

Tormey, J., 'Pursuing the Digital Pamphleteer', J. Tormey, G. Whitely, eds., *Art, Politics, and the Pamphleteer*, (Bloomsbury Academic, 2021), pp. 347–362.

Travis, T., 'The Women in Print Movement: History and Implications', *Book History*, Vol. 11 (2008), pp. 275–300.

Tufekci, Z., *Twitter and Tear Gas: The Power and Fragility of Networked Protest*, (Yale University Press, 2017).

Tuvel, R., 'In Defense of Transracialism', *Hypatia: A Journal of Feminist Philosophy*, Vol. 32/2 (Spring 2017), pp. 263–278.

United Nations, *Universal Declaration of Human Rights*, www.un.org/en/about-us/universal-declaration-of-human-rights.

United Nations Economic and Social Council, 'Study on the Problem of Discrimination Against Indigenous Populations', 12 July 1982. www.un.org/esa/socdev/unpfii/documents/MCS_xix_en.pdf.

Wachsberger, K., 'Foreword', in K. Wachsberger, ed., *Insider Histories of the Vietnam Era Underground Press*, Vol. 1, (Michigan State University Press, 2011), pp. xiii–xv.

Walker, R., 'Becoming the 3rd Wave', *Ms.* (Magazine), Spring 2002; Vol. 12, No.2, pp. 86–87.

Warner, M., *Publics and Counterpublics*, (Zone Books, 2002).

Warner, M., 'Publics and Counterpublics', *Public Culture* Vol. 14, No.1 (2002), pp. 49–90.

Weber, M., *Economy and Society*, vol. 2, ed. G. Roth and C. Wittrich, (University of California Press, 1978).

Wellman, J., *The Road to Seneca Falls: Elizabeth Cady Stanton and the First Woman's Right Convention*, (University of Illinois Press, 2004).

White, H., *Metahistory: The Historical Imagination in Nineteenth-Century Europe*, (Johns Hopkins University Press, 2014).

Whiteley, G., 'The Allure of *Pamphilos*: The Radical Art of Pamphleteering', in J. Tormey, G. Whiteley, eds., *Art, Politics, and The Pamphleteer*, (Bloomsbury Academic, 2021), pp. 5–28.

Williams, R. N., *The New Exiles: American War Resisters in Canada*, (Liveright, 1971).

Winter, M., *Finance, Commerce, and Politics in Seventeenth-Century England: The Case of Thompson and Company 1671–1678*, (University of Sheffield, 2020).

Wittstock, L. W., E. J. Salinas, 'A Brief History of the American Indian Movement', www.aimovement.org/ggc/history.html.

Wolin, S., *Politics and Vision: Continuity and Innovation in Western Political Thought*, (Princeton University Press, 2016).

Wood, G. S., *The American Revolution: A History*, (Modern Library, 2002).

World Health Organization, 'Immunizing the public against misinformation' (World Health Organization, 2020). www.who.int/news-room/feature-stories/detail/immunizing-the-public-against-misinformation.

Yang, K., *Analysing Intersectionality: A Toolbox of Methods*, (Sage, 2023).

Young, R. J., *Power and Pleasure: Louis Barthou and the Third French Republic*, (McGill-Queen's University Press, 1991).

Zedong, M., 'Letter to Chen Boda, February 1, 1939', in S. R. Schram, ed., *Mao Zedong, Mao's Road to Power: Revolutionary Writings, 1912–1949*, Volume VII, *New Democracy: 1939–1941*, (M. E. Sharpe, 2004), p. 22.

Acknowledgement

I am indebted to Corinne Hundleby for proofreading this text, to Renate Krakowczyk for her support at the Ludwig Maximilian University of Munich, and to David Bebnowski, Sakina Shakil Gröppmaier, Florian Zappe, and Gregory Jones-Katz for their support and friendship, as well as for their contribution to the ERC project *The Arts of Autonomy: Pamphleteering, Popular Philology, and the Public Sphere, 1988–2018*. This book is dedicated to Marie and Pierre-Étienne with all my love.

This project has received funding from the European Research Council (ERC) under the European Union's Horizon 2020 research and innovation programme (grant agreement No 852205). This publication reflects only the author's view, and the Agency is not responsible for any use that may be made of the information it contains.

European Research Council
Established by the European Commission

Cambridge Elements

Publishing and Book Culture

SERIES EDITOR
Samantha J. Rayner
University College London

Samantha J. Rayner is Professor of Publishing and Book Cultures at UCL. She is also Director of UCL's Centre for Publishing, co-Director of the Bloomsbury CHAPTER (Communication History, Authorship, Publishing, Textual Editing and Reading) and co-Chair of the Bookselling Research Network.

ASSOCIATE EDITOR
Leah Tether
University of Bristol

Leah Tether is Professor of Medieval Literature and Publishing at the University of Bristol. With an academic background in medieval French and English literature and a professional background in trade publishing, Leah has combined her expertise and developed an international research profile in book and publishing history from manuscript to digital.

ADVISORY BOARD

Simone Murray, Monash University

Claire Squires, University of Stirling

Andrew Nash, University of London

Leslie Howsam, Ryerson University

David Finkelstein, University of Edinburgh

Alexis Weedon, University of Bedfordshire

Alan Staton, Booksellers Association

Angus Phillips, Oxford International Centre for Publishing

Richard Fisher, Yale University Press

John Maxwell, Simon Fraser University

Shafquat Towheed, The Open University

Jen McCall, Central European University Press/Amsterdam University Press

About the Series

This series aims to fill the demand for easily accessible, quality texts available for teaching and research in the diverse and dynamic fields of Publishing and Book Culture. Rigorously researched and peer-reviewed Elements will be published under themes, or 'Gatherings'. These Elements should be the first check point for researchers or students working on that area of publishing and book trade history and practice: we hope that, situated so logically at Cambridge University Press, where academic publishing in the UK began, it will develop to create an unrivalled space where these histories and practices can be investigated and preserved.

Cambridge Elements

Publishing and Book Culture

Publishing and Book History

Gathering Editor: Andrew Nash

Andrew Nash is Reader in Book History and Director of the London Rare Books School at the Institute of English Studies, University of London. He has written books on Scottish and Victorian Literature, and edited or co-edited numerous volumes including, most recently, *The Cambridge History of the Book in Britain, Volume 7* (Cambridge University Press, 2019).

Gathering Editor: Leah Tether

Leah Tether is Professor of Medieval Literature and Publishing at the University of Bristol. With an academic background in medieval French and English literature and a professional background in trade publishing, Leah has combined her expertise and developed an international research profile in book and publishing history from manuscript to digital.

Elements in the Gathering

Publication and the Papacy in Late Antique and Medieval Europe
Samu Niskanen

Publishing in Wales: Renaissance and Resistance
Jacob D. Rawlins

The People of Print: Seventeenth-Century England
Rachel Stenner, Kaley Kramer and Adam James Smith *et al.*

Publishing in a Medieval Monastery: The View from Twelfth-Century Engelberg
Benjamin Pohl

Communicating the News in Early Modern Europe
Jenni Hyde, Massimo Rospocher, Joad Raymond, Yann Ryan, Hannu Salmi and Alexandra Schäfer-Griebel

Printing Technologies and Book Production in Seventeenth-Century Japan
Peter Kornicki

Unprinted: Publication Beyond the Press
Daria Kohler and Daniel Wakelin *et al.*

Mudie's Select Library and the Shelf Life of the Nineteenth–Century Novel
Karen Wade

Transnational Crusoe, Illustration and Reading History, 1719–1722
Sandro Jung

Art Books for the People: The Origins of The Penguin Modern Painters
David Trigg

Pamphleteering: Polemic, Print, and the Infrastructure of Political Agency
Pierre-Héli Monot

A full series listing is available at: www.cambridge.org/EPBC

Printed by Integrated Books International,
United States of America